speak tenderly

PROPHETIC MINISTRY SEASONED WITH GRACE

ivan filby

Seedbed

To Kathie, Sam, and Katie

Printed in the United States of America

Cover design and layout by Strange Last Name
Page design and layout by PerfecType, Nashville, Tennessee

Filby, Ivan, 1962-
Speak tenderly : prophetic ministry seasoned with grace / Ivan Filby. - Franklin, Tennessee : Seedbed Publishing, ©2024.

pages ; cm. + 1 video disc

ISBN: 9798888000755 (paperback)
ISBN: 9798888000786 (DVD)
ISBN: 9798888000762 (epub)
ISBN: 9798888000779 (updf)
OCLC: 1438789052

1. Prophecy--Christianity. 2. Pastoral theology. 3. Gifts, Spiritual. I. Title.

BR115.P8 F54 2024 231.7/45 2024940397

SEEDBED PUBLISHING
Franklin, Tennessee
seedbed.com

CONTENTS

FOREWORD

There I was, standing in a sea of people engaged in worship, when the stranger standing next to me leaned over to say, "I have a prophetic word for you when you're ready to hear it."

Well, of course, I wanted to hear it! I wanted to hear every word he had to share. But the room was turned toward heaven, so I waited. As soon as the session concluded I turned and asked what this person might have heard on my behalf. His one-sentence reply rocked me. It would take pages to explain just how but suffice it to say that it was so remarkably unique to my life and relationship with God that there was no way it could have been a random guess. This word was a direct hit, and I immediately sensed myself as "seen" by God. I count it as one of the more profound and encouraging moments of my life in Christ.

The man who shared that word with me was Ivan Filby. Before that day, I had no idea who he was (sorry, Ivan!), but since then I've developed a deep appreciation for his spiritual sensitivity. Ivan has such humble and winsome confidence in the power of the Holy Spirit to speak in and through him like few others I've known.

Don't you long for that same grace? Aren't you hungry to hear from God? If so, I encourage you to go exploring, believing that God shows things to people he loves (and God loves us!). Your effort will be worth it. The prophetic gift connects us with the values of heaven. It changes our perspective. It isn't always comfortable, but as we practice the prophetic voice and test it against Scripture, we discover that our thinking matures. Which I suspect is the whole point. Prophecy is one way I can practice the mind of Christ as I lean into my own sanctification.

If you have resolved to grow spiritually this year, I encourage you to eagerly desire the gift of prophecy (1 Cor. 15:1). Do what it takes to learn the voice of God and trust that as he finds you faithful, you will begin to develop hungers for specific areas where God is working—in a life or maybe a whole geographic region. And you will communicate the love of God in a more compelling way than you've ever done before.

If you've picked up this book, you're on your way to that grand spiritual adventure. In Ivan Filby, you have a marvelously well-seasoned guide for this journey. Soak it all in, and trust God to use you to welcome and advance his kingdom on earth.

—Carolyn Moore
Author of *Supernatural* and *Encounter the Spirit*

INTRODUCTION

"What no eye has seen,
what no ear has heard,
and what no human mind has conceived"—
the things God has prepared for those who love him—
these are the things God has revealed to us by his Spirit.

—1 Corinthians 2:9b–10a

Have you ever wanted to do something new, but didn't know where to start? I've felt like that many times. I vividly recall when my parents gave my brother, Alan, and me our first kites. He was a year older than I, so he got the red kite, and I settled for the green one. We couldn't wait to try them out. We ran to the playing fields near our terraced home with our parents' permission. We imagined our kites swooping high in the sky. We shared the giddy excitement of children expecting fun and adventure.

Half an hour later, we plodded home, failures. We thought anyone could fly a kite; it said so on the packaging—"easy to fly." Despite our running, shouting, and mutual blame-throwing, our kites bounced along the ground. Not even we, rather expert fibbers, thought we could convince our parents we had a successful day.

A week later, we returned, this time with an older friend. He seemed to know what he was doing. First, he licked his fingers and held them up in the air.

"Why are you doing that?" I asked.

"So I know which way the wind is blowing," he replied.

I licked my fingers and held them up too. Sure enough, one side of my fingers felt colder than the other. I now knew the direction of the wind. I knew we needed the wind to fly our kites, but I still needed to learn why the direction of the wind was important.

"Run into the wind," my friend told me, "or you'll never get your kite into the air."

It was as simple as that: we ran into the wind, and our red and green kites whooshed into the sky. We were now kite-flyers.

Some fifty years later, as I scan the soars and crashes of my life, I see this episode as metaphorical. Manufacturers built my kite with a singular purpose: to fly. Similarly, God lovingly created me with one goal: to love him and respond to his good plans for my life. Yet, like my first kite-flying attempts, I've often felt confused, unsure of why things are not working out as I had hoped, and in need of a word of comfort, clarity, or instruction. I'm sure you've experienced this confusion too.

Since becoming a Jesus-follower in 1980, I have never doubted God has good plans for me. Like many, I am encouraged by Jeremiah 29:11: "'For I know the plans I have for you,' declares the LORD, 'plans to prosper you and not to harm you, plans to give you hope and a future.'"

Yet, if I'm honest, I confess that there are times when I can make neither head nor tail of these plans. Try as I might, I can't figure out what God is doing or how I should respond. Theologians, ministers, and laypeople have wrestled with these thoughts throughout the ages. If we are honest, we all grapple with these questions to a greater or lesser extent. And, as much as we want simple answers, an easy-to-follow, step-by-step assembly guide to life eludes us. *What about the Bible?* I hear you say. *Isn't that our guide?* Well, yes and no. The Bible gives us great counsel and wisdom. It is a God-breathed compilation of histories, poetry, prophecy, biographies, letters, and apocalyptic revelations. And, as Paul writes, Scripture "is useful for teaching, rebuking, correcting and training in righteousness, so that the servant of God may be thoroughly equipped for every good work" (2 Tim. 3:16–17). The Bible equips, trains, and encourages us to follow God and love our neighbors. But search as we might, it doesn't explicitly help us to know which job to accept, whom to marry, or whether we should live in Dallas, Dubai, or Dublin.

Fortunately, God has not left us alone to figure out these questions. He has sent us his Spirit to guide us. In 1 Corinthians 2:9–12, the apostle Paul encourages us to believe that the Holy Spirit can and does guide us in God's ways for our lives:

> "What no eye has seen,
> what no ear has heard,
> and what no human mind has conceived"—
> the things God has prepared for those who
> love him—
> these are the things God has revealed to us by
> his Spirit.
>
> The Spirit searches all things, even the deep things of God. For who knows a person's thoughts except their own Spirit within them? In the same way no one knows the thoughts of God except the Spirit of God. What we have received is not the spirit of

> the world, but the Spirit who is from God, so we may understand what God has freely given us.

We can't figure out God's plans through our senses, emotions, or intellect alone, and we don't have to. Paul reminds us that the Holy Spirit, who searches the deep thoughts of the Godhead, helps us understand God's plan for us. The Spirit can reveal the things God has freely given to us.

That's good news; no, it's excellent news! But here are the questions: How does the Holy Spirit reveal God's plans to us? How does he help us understand what God has freely given to us? What hinders us from hearing, understanding, or following God's good plans?

I've written this book to help us grapple with these and other questions. Just as I needed my friend's help to get my kite into the air, I hope to be your friend as you deepen your fellowship with the Holy Spirit. Together, we'll explore why prophetic ministry can be so transformational. Sometimes, the Holy Spirit needs only to communicate one insight or idea to help us make sense of confusing or troubling circumstances.

The Holy Spirit has used me in prophetic ministry for more than forty years. I'll share some of my experiences with you in the following chapters. I'll also point out many insights about prophetic ministry from Scripture that you may have overlooked. These will help as you allow the Holy Spirit to develop and mature your prophetic gifts.

Several book clubs and churches have adopted my first book, *Livestream: Learning to Minister in the Power of the Holy Spirit* (Seedbed, 2021). The feedback has been as I hoped: readers and book club members are deepening their fellowship with the Holy Spirit. Some readers report being used by the Holy Spirit for the first time. One participant in a book club commented:

> The book club is only in its second week, but I've just learned to invite the Holy Spirit into my life, wait, watch, listen . . . and expect to be overcome and amazed. I've experienced Him "livestreaming" into my heart, mind, and Spirit. I've learned to write down what He's showing or telling me.
>
> Monday of this week was the first day I prayed, "Come, Holy Spirit," and quietly waited. Honestly, I didn't expect much because this is so new to me. Boy, was I wrong! Soon, the Spirit was telling me about relationships I needed to mend (five, to be exact—some I'd even forgotten about). Then, the Spirit told me two things about my ministry. Based on the book, I thought the focus would be on ministry, including healing. It's clear to me, though, that my priority is those five

> relationships. Yesterday, the Spirit gave me more, and today, a little more. Even more amazing is that I've fallen completely in love with the Holy Spirit in only two days. I think of Him as having all the attributes of Father God and Messiah Jesus and plenty of His own.
>
> My goal has seismically shifted from enhancing my understanding of and relationship with God to positively impacting His Kingdom.

Other readers discover they have heard from the Holy Spirit for some time, but didn't realize it! For example, one southern Vermont book club member wrote:

> As I reflect on past experiences, I realize that the Holy Spirit was talking to me, and I didn't realize it. Most of the time, the messages I received made perfect sense, and I acted on it. The book study explained a lot and helped clarify how I should respond to these messages in the future.

The book has helped reassure other readers that they are not crazy! A member of the Seedbed summer book club commented:

> I AM SO, SO GRATEFUL for the coaching of this book! I am in tears as Ivan confirms I am

> not crazy, just having a unique experience with livestreaming. I am encouraged and emboldened to tune back in and TRUST the Good Father who trusts me to pass on good gifts to His children. What a privilege! My Father lets me take the balloons and big check to the door of His kids and say, "You won! You are so amazingly beloved! Here is a life-changing gift for you!!" Oh, my King. You are amazing!

I hope these testimonies whet your appetite for what the Holy Spirit is about to do as you read these pages. I want you to fall in love with the Holy Spirit again. I pray the Spirit's messages will make perfect sense to you and others. And, for sure, I pray that you'll have the opportunity to take the prophetic equivalent of balloons and a big check to God's kids and tell them, "You won! You are so amazingly beloved!" Most of all, I want you to cry with all your heart, soul, and intellect, "Oh, my King. You are amazing!"

I have organized this book in much the same way as I arranged *Livestream*, except, this time, I have divided the material into eight chapters instead of *Livestream*'s six. In chapter 1, I discuss prophetic ministry in the life of Jesus, and you'll learn that prophetic messages do not need to be long to be powerful. In chapter 2, we examine who may prophesy and things we should consider when testing prophetic messages. I reinforce this theme in chapter 3 when we discuss Paul's insistence that prophecy should focus on strengthening, encouraging, and comforting one another for the common good. Additionally, you'll learn what it means to "eagerly desire" spiritual gifts (1 Cor. 14:1) and the ultimate reward of prophetic ministry. In chapter 4, we will examine creativity in prophetic ministry. In chapter 5, I introduce three activation exercises to help you sensitize yourself to the Spirit's promptings. In chapter 6, I introduce you to spiritual forensics, a spiritual practice that helps us to learn from our encounters with the Holy Spirit. In chapter 7, I discuss the interplay between prophetic ministry and God's good plans, and how he sometimes interrupts our journeys in unusual ways. Finally, in chapter 8, I focus on prophetic ministry's role in setting us free, helping us live in freedom, and bringing freedom to others.

At the end of each chapter, there are some questions for reflection and discussion. You can respond to these questions regardless of whether you are reading through the book by yourself or as part of a Bible study or book club. As you'll see, some questions get you to think deeply about prophetic ministry, while others are activation activities to help you tune into some ways the Holy Spirit might want to fellowship with you.

1

Prophetic Ministry in the Life of Jesus

You have searched me, LORD, and you know me.
—Psalm 139:1

Prophetic ministry is a ministry in which the Holy Spirit livestreams through us one or more of the spiritual gifts of prophecy, words of knowledge, words of wisdom, or spiritual discernment. These are four of the Holy Spirit's gifts that the apostle Paul includes in his list of spiritual gifts in 1 Corinthians 12:8–10:

> To one there is given through the Spirit a message of wisdom, to another a message of knowledge by

> means of the same Spirit, to another faith by the same Spirit, to another gifts of healing by that one Spirit, to another miraculous powers, to another prophecy, to another distinguishing between spirits, to another speaking in different kinds of tongues, and to still another the interpretation of tongues.

While I will focus more on prophecy, words of wisdom, and knowledge, you will see how prophetic ministry can release other spiritual gifts such as healing, miracles, teaching, leadership, and generosity. We see this clearly in Jesus's ministry.

Prophetic Ministry in the Life of Jesus

Jesus's prophetic ministry clearly illustrates how a simple word can awaken people's hearts and make way for remarkable transformation. Take, for example, Jesus's first encounter with Nathanael in John 1:43–51:

> The next day Jesus decided to leave for Galilee. Finding Philip, he said to him, "Follow me."
>
> Philip, like Andrew and Peter, was from the town of Bethsaida. Philip found Nathanael and

> told him, "We have found the one Moses wrote about in the Law, and about whom the prophets also wrote—Jesus of Nazareth, the son of Joseph."
>
> "Nazareth! Can anything good come from there?" Nathanael asked.
>
> "Come and see," said Philip.
>
> When Jesus saw Nathanael approaching, he said of him, "Here truly is an Israelite in whom there is no deceit."
>
> "How do you know me?" Nathanael asked.
>
> Jesus answered, "I saw you while you were still under the fig tree before Philip called you."
>
> Then Nathanael declared, "Rabbi, you are the Son of God; you are the king of Israel."
>
> Jesus said, "You believe because I told you I saw you under the fig tree. You will see greater things than that." He then added, "Very truly I tell you, you will see 'heaven open, and the angels of God ascending and descending on' the Son of Man."

Nathanael's first impression of Jesus was not positive. Most biblical scholars agree that Nazareth, a region of Galilee, was held in low esteem by many first-century Jews. Nathanael clearly expresses this view: "Nazareth!

Can anything good come from there?" (v. 46). However, Nathanael's orientation to Jesus is turned on its head when Jesus livestreams two words of knowledge. The first concerned Nathanael's character: "Here truly is an Israelite in whom there is no deceit" (v. 47). The second identifies Nathanael's whereabouts before Philip calls him: "I saw you while you were still under the fig tree before Philip called you" (v. 48b).

We can learn much from Nathanael's response. It's interesting, for example, that Nathanael doesn't respond by saying, "How do you know that *about* me?" Instead, he says, "How do you know me?" (v. 48a). There's a world of difference between knowing about someone and intimately knowing them. Prophetic ministry powerfully communicates that God knows and loves us.

It's also interesting that Nathanael doesn't rush around town telling people the new prophet thinks he's hot property. Not at all. Nathanael's response is not a navel-gazing turning in on himself, but a Jesus-gazing turning to God in worship: "Rabbi, you are the Son of God; you are the king of Israel" (v. 49).

Nathanael experienced what many of us know. When we feel known and loved by God, we can lower our emotional defenses, look outward, and see God in new and profound ways. We ought not to be surprised that Nathanael responds to Jesus's word of knowledge with a recognition that Jesus is the Son of God.

It's worth noting that Jesus doesn't have to say much to Nathanael for him to feel known. Jesus doesn't need to rehearse all the critical facts of Nathanael's life, his birth date, where he lived, or the name of his first donkey. All that is needed are two short sentences about Nathanael's character and a fig tree. In prophetic ministry, words, pictures, or actions are the vehicles the Holy Spirit uses to minister deeply to us. And, because of the Holy Spirit's ministry, we feel known by God. The apostle Paul comments on this deep Spirit-to-spirit knowing in Romans 8:16 when he writes: "The Spirit himself testifies with our spirit that we are God's children."

We must be careful if we think prophetic ministry is only about words, pictures, or actions. What we communicate is essential, but more crucial is the anointing of the Holy Spirit. In prophetic ministry, the Holy Spirit works at a depth often hidden from the minister and the person receiving prayer. During ministry time, the Holy Spirit shakes the kaleidoscopic fragments of our lives into a beautiful mosaic with Jesus at its center. It's no wonder that a timely prophetic word or insight often results in intimate worship experiences.

Jesus's encounter with Nathanael has even more to teach us. Did you notice that Nathanael's worship leads to further revelation? Jesus responds to Nathanael's exclamation—"you are the Son of God" (v. 49)—with a proclamation that Nathanael would "see 'heaven open, and the angels of God ascending and descending on' the Son of Man" (v. 51).

As you mature in prophetic ministry, you'll see this four-step pattern often repeated:

1. God livestreams a few words, maybe a picture, for you to share with someone;
2. Even though you only communicate a few words, the Holy Spirit deeply ministers to the person such that the listener feels known by God. The Holy Spirit's ministry is often beautiful and overwhelming. Tears are not uncommon;
3. Intimacy with the Holy Spirit leads us to worship; and
4. Worship leads to more revelation.

If you minister prophetically, look for additional revelation following a worshipful response. Similarly, if you have received a prophetic insight that moves you to worship, ask the Lord if he has anything else to share. He might well do.

Prophetic Ministry at the Well

A second example is helpful. Let's look at Jesus's conversation with the Samaritan woman beside Jacob's well at Sychar (John 4:7–42). Here's the context: Jesus passes through Samaria on his way from Judea to Galilee. He's tired and hungry, and while his disciples head into town to buy food, he sits beside Jacob's well to rest. A local woman turns up at an unusual time to draw water and carry it home in the heat of the noonday sun. He's thirsty and asks the woman for water. What follows is a fascinating conversation about living water and proper worship.

Unexpectedly, there's a dramatic shift in the conversation. Jesus asks the woman to go and call her husband and return to continue the discussion. She admits she is not married, and Jesus gives her a word of knowledge containing just three facts: (1) you are correct; you have no husband, (2) you've had five previous husbands, and (3) the man with whom you currently live is not your husband.

The conversation continues. What happens next is fascinating and instructive. Let's read John 4:28–29 together: "Then, leaving her water jar, the woman went back to the town and said to the people, 'Come, see a man who told me everything I ever did. Could this be the Messiah?'" Isn't it fascinating that Jesus only communicates three facts?

Still, the woman declares that Jesus told her *everything* she ever did.

After ministry time, someone occasionally says, "You read my mail." A person communicating words of knowledge might share only one fact, sometimes two or three, but rarely more, but enough for the person to feel *known* by God. But that's hardly reading their mail. If someone read your mail, they'd know what's on your bank statement, the local pizza company's special offers, and the most recent news from your local charities. People sometimes assume that the minister knows everything about them because the Holy Spirit livestreams a snippet of information. Rest assured; this is not the case. The Holy Spirit is not in the gotcha business, trying to expose or shame people. Instead, the Holy Spirit is in the I've-got-something-better-for-you business. The Spirit works alongside the Father and the Son on your healing, holiness, and wholeness so that you, in turn, can minister his love and power more effectively to others.

Interestingly, the prophetic livestream with the Samaritan woman flows during a random conversation; not in a synagogue, but during an everyday task. Jesus doesn't start the conversation with, "Hey, woman, I know a ton of stuff about you." No, he starts having a conversation with her about water. Perhaps the Holy Spirit didn't livestream information about her marital history until well into the conversation. We don't know for sure, but this is often how prophetic ministry works. What starts as small talk becomes supercharged with possibilities as the Holy Spirit joins in.

Jesus's encounter with the woman at the well has much more to teach us about prophetic ministry. The Samaritan woman turns up at Jacob's well at noon, an unusual time for carrying heavy water jugs. We can speculate why she comes at this time of day, but we don't know for sure. I've discovered that noticing a person's unusual word choices, actions, or even clothing sensitizes me to the possibility that the Holy Spirit might want to communicate something to them. Suppose the number of buttons on someone's coat sleeve, the color of their glasses, scuffs on shoes, or how they walk catches my eye. In that case, I'll often ask the Holy Spirit if what I see is a ministry launching point.

For example, I was ministering in Delft, a beautiful old city in the Netherlands, when the Spirit drew my attention to one woman's eyes. When I prayed with her, I had the impression that I should tell her, "God has seen how you use your eyes to attract men, and he will now use them to draw people to himself." I wanted to know how the word might be meaningful. I learned later that this woman was a prostitute working in the windows in the Amsterdam Red Light district, where she used eye contact to attract customers. God knew how significant the woman's eyes were to her trade, and he spoke to her powerfully, offering her a way to redirect her life. Had the Spirit not drawn my attention to her eyes, I may have missed this ministry opportunity.

Jesus notices the woman drawing water at an unusual time, and begins his conversation using water as the theme. He asks, "Will you give me a drink?" (v. 7).

The conversation goes a little deeper: "If you knew the gift of God and who it is that asks you for a drink, you would have asked him and he would have given you living water" (v. 10).

Then, deeper still: "Everyone who drinks this water will be thirsty again, but whoever drinks the water I give them will never thirst. Indeed, the water I give them will become in them a spring of water welling up to eternal life" (vv. 13–14).

These are mind-boggling revelations, but they leave the woman unchanged. Isn't that interesting? Jesus is, without question, the best teacher who has ever walked on earth. He's a better teacher than the best-selling authors we all love; better than every megachurch pastor; better than Luther, Calvin, and Wesley combined. He's certainly a better teacher than you or I. Yet, the woman doesn't comment on his teaching at all. She remembers Jesus's prophetic insight: "Come, see a man who told me everything I ever did" (v. 29).

Now let's consider the impact of Jesus's prophetic ministry to this woman on her community. John 4:39–41 is fascinating: "Many of the Samaritans from that town believed in him because of the woman's testimony, 'He told me everything I ever did.' So when the Samaritans came to him, they urged him to stay with them, and he stayed two days. And because of his words many more became believers."

Jesus's words of knowledge about the woman's domestic relationships convince the woman about Jesus. Her testimony convinces many in the Samaritan community to believe in him and inspires them to invite Jesus to stay to get to know him better. Jesus stays with them for two additional days. As people listen to Jesus, many more put their faith in him.

Now, let's look at verse 42: "They said to the woman, 'We no longer believe just because of what you said; now we have heard for ourselves, and we know that this man really is the Savior of the world.'"

All this happened because Jesus livestreamed three facts to a random woman. His prophetic insight opened the woman's heart. She told her community about her encounter with Jesus. Because of her testimony, her community visited with Jesus and invited him to stay. It was only then that the Samaritan community listened to Jesus's teaching. Prophetic insights open conversations and ministry opportunities that otherwise would never have happened.

You might well ask what was remarkable about these insights. Jesus, after all, was the Son of God, and God, by his very nature, would know all this stuff, wouldn't he? That would be true had Jesus not voluntarily emptied himself of his God-nature and taken on the limitations of humanity (Phil. 2:6–8). We glimpse these limitations during Jesus's betrayal in the garden. Judas betrays Jesus with a kiss. When the crowd, armed with swords and clubs, steps forward to seize Jesus, one of Jesus's companions retaliates, cutting off the high priest's servant's ear. Jesus responds, constrained by his human limitations, setting aside what he could have done: "'Put your sword back in its place,' Jesus said to him, 'for all who draw the sword will die by the sword. Do you think I cannot call on my Father, and he will at once put at my disposal more than twelve legions of angels? But how then would the Scriptures be fulfilled that say it must happen in this way?'" (Matt. 26:52–54).

I have yet to learn how many angels are in one legion, let alone twelve. If one standard Roman legion had approximately four thousand foot soldiers, we might speculate that there are almost fifty thousand angels in twelve. But however many there are, we know there would be enough to take down the Romans, the chief priests, elders, the armed mob, and the whole kit and caboodle. Had Jesus asked, his Father would have sent these reinforcements. But Jesus didn't ask. He lived his life constrained by the human limitations that constrain us all.

Here's the point: Jesus's divinity didn't give him any shortcuts in prophetic ministry. He had to watch what the Father was doing and listen to the Spirit's voice, just like you and I. For sure, his sinlessness would have made it easier to see and hear, but he got no other breaks. Every prophetic insight Jesus gave was livestreamed through fellowshipping with the Holy Spirit. He invites us to do the same.

The Cry of Your Heart

Prophetic ministry can help a person feel known by God—a reality as wonderful today as it was in New Testament times. For example, in 1985, I lived in Bourneville, a suburb of the city of Birmingham in England, best known for being the headquarters of the chocolate manufacturer Cadbury. If you are a chocolate-lover, this is a fantastic place to live, with chocolate aromas regularly wafting over the village.

One evening I was working on my PhD dissertation, when my friend David's face kept popping into my mind. I kept trying to concentrate on my academic writing, but I could not get David's face out of my mind's eye. I saved my document, put down my books, and asked the Lord how I should pray for David. Instantly, a thought popped into my mind. I had to tell David: *The Lord has heard the cry of your heart and is answering you right now.* David lived a mile or so away in the next village. I put on my shoes, grabbed my coat and Bible, and started walking to his home.

David was new to the ministry of the Holy Spirit. The first time I visited his home, I came with a group of young people from his church, where he served as an elder. David knew the gang of teens and twentysomethings accompanying me; I was the only stranger. During the evening, Emily, one of the teenage girls, told the group about her chronic head and neck pains. My friend Martin asked me to pray for her healing. I had hardly begun to pray, when the Holy Spirit came on Emily so powerfully that she fell backward onto the living room carpet. None of us had expected this to happen. Emily was stunned, maybe literally, by the power of God. She quickly stood up, telling everyone that the headache and neck pain she had experienced to a greater or lesser extent for several months had instantly gone.

Emily was ecstatic, but the rest of the room went quiet. This unexpected healing put David in a difficult position. He was the elder of a cessationist church that believed the gifts of the Holy Spirit had passed away with the apostles. Many people hold this theological position. It's a much harder position to maintain when the Holy Spirit heals one of your daughter's friends three feet in front of you in your living room.

David faced a dilemma. Either he had to discount Emily's healing (which Emily, rather inconveniently, kept insisting was real), or he had to change his theological position. To his credit, he changed his theology and was soon ministering in the Spirit's power himself. David and I became good friends.

It took me twenty minutes or so to walk to his house. During that time, I asked the Lord for more information on the "cry" of David's heart. Silence. Nada. Zilch! When I knocked on his door, I still had no idea what was disturbing David.

David opened his front door, smiled, and said in his rather proper English accent, "Ivan! Jolly good to see you. Do come in." David made us two cups of tea, and we chatted in his lounge. During our catch-up conversation, I told him about the impression the Holy Spirit had given me earlier that evening.

"I have no idea what this means, David," I said, "but I keep getting the impression I must tell you that 'The Lord has heard the cry of your heart and is answering you right now.' Does that mean anything to you?"

David let out a very audible sigh of relief. He beamed, "That's a huge answer to prayer." But my friend remained silent on the significance of those words.

A year or so later, when we were sipping tea, this time in his kitchen, David told me more. "Ivan, do you remember when you called around one evening last year to let me know the impression you had? You know, when you told me the Lord had heard the cry of my heart? Let me tell you about it. I was due to have minor surgery under a full anesthetic later that week. I'd read that when people regain consciousness after an anesthetic, they sometimes curse and say all sorts of things they regret. Before I knew Jesus, I cursed like a trooper. I was worried I'd say terrible things as the anesthetic wore off and ruin my Christian testimony. As silly as it might seem, I was more worried about what I might say in the recovery room than about the surgery itself. When you told me that 'the Lord had heard the cry of my heart and was answering me right now,' a huge wave of peace flooded me. I knew God had heard my prayer."

Fast-forward five years to 1990. I was now living in Dublin, Ireland, and had only been attending Maranatha

Christian Fellowship for just a few weeks. On Easter Sunday, just as the service was closing, Pastor Mark Habgood stood up. He announced that he believed the Holy Spirit wanted to do more that day, and invited anyone who wanted prayer to remain for a time of ministry. Remarkably, most of the hundred or so church members stayed, probably leading to some burnt Sunday lunches. These people were so hungry for the Holy Spirit. To my surprise, Pastor Mark said, "I want to spend time praying with everyone who has stayed for ministry." He paused and continued, "Ivan Filby will join me." His invitation was unplanned. I was a recent addition to the congregation; I certainly hadn't expected an invitation to join the pastor in a time of ministry. I walked to the front of the auditorium, and we began our ministry time.

An hour later, we must have prayed and given prophetic words to fifty or sixty people, maybe more. As our ministry time was closing, I noticed the musicians who had played quietly in the background for the last hour. I had met the guitarists before, but this was the first time I had seen the keyboard player. As I prayed for the person in front of me, the Holy Spirit livestreamed a brief message for the keyboardist. I had the strongest impression I needed to tell her: *God has heard the cry of your heart and is answering you right now.*

I gave the final guy I was praying with some post-ministry advice, then approached the now sore-fingered musician. I shared my prophetic impression with her while she continued to play, and then walked away to rejoin Pastor Mark. I didn't give this prophetic message much thought, except to wonder whether the keyboard player had some surgery scheduled soon. It was just one of many prophetic words I'd shared during the ministry time.

I didn't know that the keyboard player had just returned from six weeks in San Francisco. During that time, the Lord repeatedly told her: *Prepare for marriage*. This impression made no sense to her as she wasn't dating. During every prayer time, the Holy Spirit gave her the same notion: *Prepare for marriage.* The impression increased when she returned to Dublin and visited her prayer spot on Killiney Hill. She was confused and frustrated. "God," she pleaded, "either show me whom you are leading me to or quit bringing up the subject."

When I gave her the prophetic message, *God has heard the cry of your heart and is answering you right now*, she took one look at me and knew I would be her husband! She even went home and wrote my name in her journal, confident that God was bringing us together. I, of course, knew none of this at all.

However, a few days later, we were both invited for dinner by a group of mutual friends. We chatted and arranged to meet for coffee later in the week. Kathie and I married fifteen months later. God is good.

While these stories are very different, they share some commonalities. I had the same prophetic message for both David and Kathie: *God has heard the cry of your heart and is answering you right now*. In both instances, I was unaware of their concerns. All I knew was that God had heard the cry of each person's heart and wanted them to know he was answering them at that very moment. I left each ministry experience none the wiser about the significance of the message. David didn't tell me about his concern for a full twelve months. It took Kathie several months before she showed me her journal entry, naming me as her future husband. Yet, in both cases, God did something remarkable. A deep peace flooded David's soul when I shared my impression with him. And what can I say? Kathie fell in love with me when I gave her the same message! That was the most life-changing and expensive prophetic word I have ever given!

Interestingly, neither prophetic message included any convincing personal information. If anything, the insights seemed rather vague, a message I might have given to anyone. Nevertheless, God used the remarkable timing of each word to convince David and Kathie that he knew them.

This Is Me

One of our deepest needs as humans is to be known. Someone who cheers us on without knowing us is a fan. And, while fans might be fun, they come and go. What we want, what we crave, is to be known, warts and all, and still loved unconditionally.

One of the consequences of sin is that we hide. As soon as Adam and Eve recognized they had rebelled from God, they hid, first from each other and then from God (Genesis 3:7–8). The mercilessness of sin is that our longing to be fully known and loved has not lessened, but our sin-derived sense that we are inadequate, or never enough, results in us hiding from the very ones we want to know and love us the very most.

Jesus is good news. He still speaks tender words of grace, forgiveness, reconciliation, and hope to our troubled souls. He invites us to do the same.

Two of the biggest-selling songs in recent years are about our desire to be authentically known: "This Is Me" from *The Greatest Showman* and Lauren Daigle's "You Say."

People have downloaded these songs hundreds of millions of times. The words of an earlier, more enduring songwriter are even more helpful in our quest. Consider David's lyrics from his song about being known by God. We've lost the original melody, but we can still find the lyrics in the first few verses of Psalm 139. Read them aloud with me:

> You have searched me, Lord,
>   and you know me.
> You know when I sit and when I rise;
>   you perceive my thoughts from afar.
> You discern my going out and my lying down;
>   you are familiar with all my ways.
> Before a word is on my tongue
>   you, Lord, know it completely.
> You hem me in behind and before,
>   and you lay your hand upon me.
> Such knowledge is too wonderful for me,
>   too lofty for me to attain. (vv. 1–6)

It's worth pausing here to count the number of times words like *know*, *searched*, *perceive*, *familiar*, or *discern* are used in this passage. I counted seven. David is not referring to an "I've got eyes in the back of my head; stop messing around, class," old schoolteacher type of knowing. No, David's talking about a loving parent celebrating every second of their child's life. Gazing lovingly into the child's face, our heavenly Father whispers, "I'm here for you, I love you, and I'll never leave you."

Only as we receive this love do we understand who we really are. Only then can we authentically say, *This is me.* Only then do we dare finish David's song:

> Search me, God, and know my heart;
>   test me and know my anxious thoughts.
> See if there is any offensive way in me,
>   and lead me in the way everlasting. (vv. 23–24)

Questions for Reflection and Discussion

1. Meditate on Jeremiah 29:11: "'For I know the plans I have for you,' declares the Lord, 'plans to prosper you and not to harm you, plans to give you hope and a future.'" Think back over your life. How have you seen the Lord guiding you and leading you? On a scale of 1–10, how confident are you that God has good things for you in the future? Be honest. Invite God into this conversation, letting him know your hopes and fears.

2. In John 1:46, we see Nathanael stating: "Nazareth! Can anything good come from there?" What do people say

about your city, town, or village? Sit quietly and ask the Lord what he feels about your town. Write any impressions that come to you over the next twenty-four hours and use them as a prayer focus.

3. Can you identify other examples from Scripture where Jesus used prophetic ministry to reveal God's heart? Who was Jesus talking to? What happened?

4. Read Psalm 139. What have been the times in your life when you most profoundly experienced that God knew and loved you? What happened? How did God communicate his love for you?

5. Reread Psalm 139, paying attention to your emotions as you read. What do you feel as you read this psalm? You may possibly feel overwhelmed with joy, or maybe you feel angry if, at times, it appears as if God has not been present. Perhaps you feel ashamed or hopeful. Name your emotions and tell God how you feel in a prayer.

2

Building Firm Foundations for Prophetic Ministry

Do not treat prophecies with contempt but test them all; hold on to what is good.

—1 Thessalonians 5:20–21

Over the years, I have hired many people: administrators, academics, vice presidents, and presidents. Finding the right candidate possessing the technical and people skills your organization needs is both an art and a science. Hiring a poor fit can be costly, and managers do all they can to minimize the likelihood of selecting the wrong candidate. If you have worked in human resources, you'll know that an organization thinks about the type of person they want to hire long before they invite anyone to a job interview. Often, the search process begins by crafting two documents: a job description and a person specification. The job description identifies the job holder's task, while the person specification describes the ideal candidate's qualifications, experience, and character. Suppose an organization posted a job opportunity for a receptionist. In that case, the job description might include the ability to answer the phone and work with various software packages. The person specification might mention the ideal candidate's ability to work with people, handle pressure, communicate clearly, and have experience working in similar environments.

While Paul would never have heard the term *person specification*, he clearly understood the concept. In 1 Timothy 3:1–7, Paul lists the behavioral and character qualities a church should look for when selecting its elders. Here is Paul's person specification for a church overseer:

> Here is a trustworthy saying: Whoever aspires to be an overseer desires a noble task. Now the overseer is to be above reproach, faithful to his wife, temperate, self-controlled, respectable, hospitable, able to teach, not given to drunkenness, not violent but gentle, not quarrelsome, not a lover of money. He must manage his own family well and

> see that his children obey him, and he must do so in a manner worthy of full respect. (If anyone does not know how to manage his own family, how can he take care of God's church?) He must not be a recent convert, or he may become conceited and fall under the same judgment as the devil. He must also have a good reputation with outsiders, so that he will not fall into disgrace and into the devil's trap.

Before moving on, count the standards Paul enumerates. Don't rush ahead and skip on; go back and count the number of criteria Paul uses in his person specification. It's important.

How many did you count? I counted seventeen. Let's list them out.

An overseer must:

1. be above reproach
2. be faithful to one's spouse
3. be temperate
4. be self-controlled
5. be respectable
6. be hospitable
7. be able to teach
8. not be given to drunkenness

9. not be violent
10. be gentle
11. not be quarrelsome
12. not be a lover of money
13. be able to manage one's household well
14. have obedient children
15. not be a recent convert
16. not become conceited
17. have a good reputation

For an early person specification, that's very comprehensive. But Paul's not done. After listing the qualities a church should expect from overseers, Paul writes his person specification for deacons. You can read these for yourself in 1 Timothy 3:8–13.

Now compare Paul's person specification for overseers with qualities he looks for in those manifesting the Holy Spirit's gifts. See if you can count the qualities Paul lists in 1 Corinthians 12:7–11:

> Now to each one the manifestation of the Spirit is given for the common good. To one there is given through the Spirit a message of wisdom, to another a message of knowledge by means of the same Spirit, to another faith by the same Spirit, to another gifts of healing by that one Spirit, to another miraculous

> powers, to another prophecy, to another distinguishing between spirits, to another speaking in different kinds of tongues, and to still another the interpretation of tongues. All these are the work of one and the same Spirit, and he distributes them to each one, just as he determines.

How many did you count? One, two, maybe three? Read the scripture once more to ensure you didn't miss any. How many did you spot? What's your total?

I didn't count any, not a single one. I find that curious because I hear people list criteria all the time. I regularly overhear comments like, "I'm not good enough; the Holy Spirit would never choose me," or "I have other gifts; I'm just not anointed this way." I sometimes hear the authenticity of spiritual gifts questioned because they happen in a Catholic, Baptist, Presbyterian, Methodist, or independent church.

The inclusivity of Holy Spirit ministry echoes the passage from the prophet Joel that Peter quotes on the day of Pentecost. We read it in Acts 2:17–18: "'In the last days, God says, I will pour out my Spirit on all people. Your sons and daughters will prophesy, your young men will see visions, your old men will dream dreams. Even on my servants, both men and women, I will pour out my Spirit in those days, and they will prophesy.'"

Joel includes men and women, old folk and young guns, family insiders, and, shockingly, servants too. This promise differs radically from the Old Testament norm, where only prophets, priests, and kings were filled with the Holy Spirit. God desires that we all enjoy the fullness of the Holy Spirit so that we, in turn, can minister his grace to others.

The problem is that we consciously or unconsciously add to Paul's list. In our minds, we rewrite the list to read something like:

> Now, to one super-spiritual person, the manifestation of the Spirit is given for the common good; to another fifth-generation pastor's kid, there is given through the Spirit a message of wisdom; to another apostle or prophet, a message of knowledge by means of the same Spirit; to another most reverend holier-than-thou Joe or Josephine [apologies if these are your names], faith by the same Spirit; or, to still another unbelievably anointed TV evangelist, gifts of healing by that one Spirit.

Paul, who knew about person specifications, didn't list any of these. Why? Because the Spirit manifests gifts to *each one*. When Paul writes "each one" (1 Cor. 12:11), he means each one, *everyone*. God does not call everyone to be an overseer, even though, as Paul writes, it is a "noble task" (1 Tim. 3:1). He, therefore, writes down essential criteria to help churches make wise leadership choices. He doesn't need to write down any requirements for using spiritual gifts because we all have a part to play.

The scripture says *to one, to another*, and *to still another*. There are no special qualifications for livestreaming the gifts of the Holy Spirit. You're hired if you are a Jesus-follower and want to bless others! The job is yours. The only caveat Paul mentions is that the manifestations of the Spirit are given *for the common good* (1 Cor. 12:7). The Holy Spirit empowers us so we can all benefit. It's as if God is giving a divine jigsaw puzzle and telling us we must play together to see this fuller picture of God's majesty, power, and love. That's why we all need to play our part.

That's good news!

Learning to Minister with Grace

Learning to prophesy is like playing a fretless stringed instrument such as a violin or double bass. When we are starting, we often need to correct some notes. It takes time and practice to position our fingers correctly on the fingerboard and simultaneously bow with the correct pressure on the strings. We initially learned to play by reading sheet music. Once we have mastered playing technique and some music theory, we can learn to improvise.

Unless you are an exceptional musician, you'll have to endure plenty of squeaks and squawks, flat notes, and sharp notes, before your musical playing begins. So will your parents and neighbors! But that's the only way to learn. The same is true in prophetic ministry. Some people receive an unusual anointing and minister in power and accuracy right from the get-go. Most of us, however, must practice and learn, hopefully, in a safe and encouraging environment.

In the early days of my prophetic ministry, I thought of myself as a surgeon with a sharp prophetic scalpel. The Holy Spirit often would give me a glimpse of who a person could be, and I too readily cut and sliced without much anesthetic to expose and remove whatever was hindering them. I had ample prophetic salt to throw on the open wound to help the healing process—or so I thought. I don't doubt that the insights came from the Lord, but I wish I'd had a better bedside manner. There is undoubtedly a time and place for salt in prophetic ministry, but it is much rarer than I imagined. Nowadays, instead of salt, I pray my life will be seasoned with grace. Thankfully, some older leaders helped me. Not all were powerfully prophetic, but all were wise. And they helped me find better ways to communicate the prophetic insights I received with increasing regularity. I now have the privilege of assisting others to learn from my experiences and mistakes.

Prophecy as Contested Terrain

More than likely, if you lived in the USA during recent presidential elections, you'll be aware of how divisive public prophecy has become. One group of prophets proclaimed one presidential candidate as God's chosen instrument, while other prophetic groups contested this claim. Confusing, eh? A casual reading of the Scriptures might lead us to conclude that prophecy was much cleaner and clearer in Old Testament times. Yet, this was not the case. Consider, for example, the oft-quoted Scripture from Jeremiah 29:11 that I referenced in chapter 1: "'For I know the plans I have for you,' declares the LORD, 'plans to prosper you and not to harm you, plans to give you hope and a future.'"

Jeremiah wrote this in a letter to all the people in exile in Babylon. We must understand the context of Jeremiah's letter to understand this scriptural truth more completely. Jeremiah was writing to correct Hananiah's false prophecy that the Babylonian exile would be over soon. We can read Hananiah's prophetic message in Jeremiah 28:2–4:

> "This is what the LORD Almighty, the God of Israel, says: 'I will break the yoke of the king of Babylon. Within two years I will bring back to this place all the articles of the LORD's house that Nebuchadnezzar king of Babylon removed from here and took to Babylon. I will also bring back to this place Jehoiachin son of Jehoiakim king of Judah and all the other exiles from Judah who went to Babylon,' declares the LORD, 'for I will break the yoke of the king of Babylon.'"

Put yourself in the picture. Imagine you were one of the Israelites forcibly carried into exile by Nebuchadnezzar's troops. You'd long to return to Jerusalem, wouldn't you? You'd want Nebuchadnezzar to get his comeuppance; you'd like to rebuild the temple. In that context, Hananiah's prophecy would have been welcome news. Imagine the Israelites throwing private parties and dancing to chart-topping pop songs like, "We're Going Home," "Only Two More Years," and "We're Gonna Broke Nebu's Yoke"! Admittedly, the last song is not grammatically correct, but the writers struggled with the lack of vowels in ancient Hebrew and wrote the chorus after a sizeable cup of old-school grape juice!

You get the picture; Hananiah's prophecy was sweet music to enslaved Hebrew ears.

Jeremiah's letter, however, offers a very different vision of the future. He brings what, at first blush, appears to be unwelcome news: the captivity will last for seventy years, not for two, as Hananiah had prophesied. Instead of packing their bags and preparing to head to Jerusalem, he tells them to, "Build houses and settle down; plant gardens and eat what they produce. Marry and have sons and daughters; find wives for your sons and give your daughters in marriage, so that they too may have sons and daughters. Increase in number there; do not decrease" (29:5–6). Then, instead of learning the second verse of "We're Gonna Broke Nebu's Yoke," Jeremiah tells the captives: "Also, seek the peace and prosperity of the city to which I have carried you into exile. Pray to the Lord for it, because if it prospers, you too will prosper" (v. 7).

And it is in this context that God, through Jeremiah, reminds the people:

> "For I know the plans I have for you," declares the Lord, "plans to prosper you and not to harm you, plans to give you hope and a future. Then you will call on me and come and pray to me, and I will listen to you. You will seek me and find me when you seek me with all your heart. I will be found by you," declares the Lord, "and will bring you back from captivity. I will gather you from

> all the nations and places where I have banished you," declares the LORD, "and will bring you back to the place from which I carried you into exile." (vv. 11–14)

Jeremiah's prophecy, God's word, must have been less welcome, but it was nonetheless good.

Prophetic Perspective

Many people think of prophecy and foretelling almost interchangeably. They are not. Certainly, prophetic ministry, from time to time, does give us insight into the future. However, we must be cautious about how we interpret such prophetic messages. Every Christmas, for example, we marvel at Isaiah's prophecy, recorded in Isaiah 7:14–16: "Therefore the Lord himself will give you a sign: The virgin will conceive and give birth to a son, and will call him Immanuel. He will be eating curds and honey when he knows enough to reject the wrong and choose the right, for before the boy knows enough to reject the wrong and choose the right, the land of the two kings you dread will be laid waste."

I don't think Isaiah or his listeners had Jesus in mind when he prophesied. More likely, the virgin was a well-known single woman living in the region. The detail, "before the boy knows enough to reject the wrong and choose the right, the land of the two kings you dread will be laid waste," anchors Isaiah's prophecy in his own time. Only in hindsight do we see the messianic prophecy in all its glory.

In 1986, I visited a good friend in Rome. One day during prayer, I felt the Lord tell me that he would have me attend theological college to get additional training. When I landed back in the United Kingdom, I began to search for colleges. I even set up times to visit several of them. The morning of my first visit, after I left my apartment, I felt so unpeaceful that I returned home and canceled all my visits. I didn't doubt that I would attend a theological college at some point in time, but I knew it was not then.

I had heard God, but I had not understood how prophetic perspective works. I did not attend a theological college for another fourteen years. When the timing was right, I gobbled up the material and then served as a master of arts thesis grader for several years.

Our friends own a beautiful home in Estes Park, Colorado. When Kathie and I visit, we enjoy standing on their deck and looking over at the enormous mountains in Rocky Mountain National Park. Some mountains look closer than others. That's because some are closer! But others only look closer because of their comparative size. In fact, they are farther away than the smaller peaks closer to the deck. Prophecy is sometimes like this. The Holy Spirit livestreams insights that look imminent when they might be years away.

Last year I received an unexpected message from a woman I had given a prophecy to more than ten years ago. She wrote:

> I am sure you don't remember me, but you gave me a prophetic word maybe ten years ago at a pastors' retreat. I am writing to let you know how the Lord has led.
>
> You told me that God gave you my name and that you should tell me the image you saw. The image was of me listening to the heartbeat of God with a stethoscope and then writing. For the longest time, I didn't fully understand. I knew that I had always connected with the heart of God through writing, but I could tell that wasn't the whole narrative.
>
> Over the past few years, my family and I have served as missionaries in Hungary. During this time, I desperately needed a spiritual mentor. A fellow missionary recommended a spiritual director. I began meeting with her regularly.

> About half a year later, I began feeling drawn to the ministry of spiritual direction myself. When I shared with my spiritual director my desire to see what God might be stirring, I also shared with her the prophetic word you gave me a decade earlier. She smiled and said, "Spiritual Direction is often called Holy Listening."
>
> I have begun my master's certificate to become a spiritual director. I feel like God used you in a big way to help me understand the ministry that God is leading me towards.
>
> I wanted to say thank you for listening to God and sharing with me what you felt led to share. Blessings to you and your family.

In all honesty, I had forgotten this ministry encounter. That doesn't matter. What matters is that this woman didn't, and she kept prayerfully wrestling with the word for more than ten years until its meaning became more evident.

Ways to Test Prophetic Messages

In public settings, Paul writes, prophetic ministry needs to be orderly. In 1 Corinthians 14:29–33, he writes that while all can prophesy in turn, church members should only give two or three prophecies at any time. Grouping prophecies in this way allows listeners to weigh them before they forget what was said.

> Two or three prophets should speak, and the others should weigh carefully what is said. And if a revelation comes to someone who is sitting down, the first speaker should stop. For you can all prophesy in turn so that everyone may be instructed and encouraged. The spirits of prophets are subject to the control of prophets. For God is not a God of disorder but of peace—as in all the congregations of the Lord's people.

To the chagrin of many a church leader, Paul did not explicitly explain how we might carefully weigh prophetic messages. That said, I believe he gives us some clues in 1 Thessalonians 5:20–21, where he wrote: "Do not treat prophecies with contempt but test them all; hold on to what is good."

First Thessalonians was one of Paul's earliest letters, probably written between AD 49–51. We might well ask why Paul thought it necessary to instruct the church not to treat prophecies with contempt so soon after Pentecost. There were likely false prophets around. However, if this were Paul's concern, he would have written something like, "Beware of false prophets." More probably, I think, is the likelihood that a prophecy given to the church had not come true. A young prophet eager for the Lord's return may have set a date for the Second Coming. There's been plenty of those throughout church history. If this was the cause, perhaps the church threw the baby out with the bathwater, despising every prophecy that came thereafter. Paul doesn't tell the church to accept or reject every prophecy, but to test them all to see which parts of each are genuine.

Testing prophecy is like panning for gold, sifting out all the dirt from a riverbed until only the gold is left. A prophetic utterance given today is unlikely to be either 100-percent right or wrong; it's likely a mix. We must discern which part of the mix is inspired by the Holy Spirit. Even the prophet Agabus arguably got one fact wrong in his prophetic warning to Paul in Acts 16. Agabus correctly predicted Paul would be bound in Jerusalem (Acts 21:11). However, he prophesied that Jewish leaders would bind Paul when, in fact, it was the Romans who put him in chains (v. 33). Some scholars argue that prophetic utterances as well as biblical authors have some license to speak in literary, or suggestive terms—meaning, since the Jewish leaders were behind the charges against Paul, they were ultimately responsible for putting him in chains. That may be the case here. Nonetheless, even if Agabus got one point incorrect, it didn't invalidate his prophecy. It shows that even Agabus may have made an error, and we will likely do the same. Just like some teachers/preachers will make mistakes or some pastors may offer the wrong counsel occasionally, it doesn't invalidate their entire ministry office. We must carefully weigh every prophecy and hold on to what is good.

The Holy Spirit's gift of discernment is enormously helpful. Those livestreaming this gift often get a picture or a sense of unease when a word is in error or demonically inspired. The gift can help us discern the message's content and the spirit behind the inspiration. Let's see examples of each.

The account of the prophet Micaiah's encounters with Judah's king, Jehoshaphat, and Ahab, the king of Israel, in 1 Kings 22 gives an excellent example of discerning a prophecy's content. In this account, Ahab approached Jehoshaphat to discuss joining forces to fight against Ramoth Gilead. Jehoshaphat insisted on seeking the counsel of the Lord before going into battle. Ahab brought together four hundred prophets, all of whom predicted success. Jehoshaphat asked Ahab if there were any other prophets they could consult. Ahab replied that there was still one, Micaiah, "but I hate him because he never prophesies anything good about me, but always bad" (v. 8).

The kings summoned Micaiah to meet them. As he approached the kings, he saw the other four hundred prophets prophesying victory against Ramoth Gilead. He would have seen Zedekiah, one of the prophets, lifting iron horns over his head, shouting, "This is what the LORD says: 'With these, you will gore the Arameans until they are destroyed'" (v. 11).

A messenger briefed Micaiah that the other four hundred prophets had all prophesied success and to "Let your word agree with theirs, and speak favorably" (v. 13).

That's some pressure! Imagine how Micaiah must have felt. He was the four hundred and first prophet invited to prophesy. Micaiah, however, didn't buckle under the pressure. Previously, God had shown Micaiah a vision in which a deceiving spirit misled the other four hundred prophets to prophesy success for the king. Instead of predicting success, Micaiah told the kings that going to war would be disastrous for Israel (v. 23), and it was.

Wow, one deceiving spirit influenced four hundred prophets.

I have no doubt the prophets thought they were prophesying correctly. Still, they could not discern the difference between the voice of the Lord and this deceiving spirit. Only Micaiah correctly heard the Lord.

Acts 16:16–18 provides an example of Paul discerning the spirit behind the prophecy.

> Once when we were going to the place of prayer, we were met by a female slave who had a spirit by which she predicted the future. She earned a great deal of money for her owners by fortune-telling. She followed Paul and the rest of us, shouting, "These men are servants of the Most High God, who are telling you the way to be saved." She kept this up for many days. Finally Paul became so annoyed that he turned around and said to the spirit, "In the name of Jesus Christ I command you to come out of her!" At that moment the spirit left her.

Here we meet a young woman who followed Paul and Silas for days shouting out: "These men are servants of the Most High God, who are telling you how to be saved" (v. 17). She'd be a social media influencer or PR spin doctor if alive today. She kept telling everyone that Paul and Silas were "servants of the Most High God." That was true. She continued, shouting that Paul and Silas were telling people how to "be saved." That was also true.

She was loud and insistent and kept her uninvited PR campaign going for days. Surely all this free publicity and promotion must be good? Not if a fortune-telling spirit inspires it. After many days, Paul had had enough of her shouting and cast out the evil spirit in Jesus's name. The spirit left her, she lost her fortune-telling gift, her owners were upset, and Paul and Silas were soon singing hymns in prison.

Interestingly, in 1 Thessalonians 5:20–21, when Paul told us not to treat prophecies with contempt but to test them all, he didn't instruct us to hold on to what is *true*. Instead, he set a higher standard, telling us to hold on to what is *good*. We must never forget that we have an adversary who accuses us "before our God day and night" (Rev. 12:10). Likely, there is some truth in these accusations. However, Satan intended these accusations for harm, not good. God wants only good for us, and he instructs us to get a firm grip on that.

Only some have discernment gifts. How do we carefully weigh prophecies without this gift? Many church leaders, including myself, at times, find this problematic. A good starting point is to consider who is giving the prophecy and how they give it. Paul gives us some clues in the verses leading up to his exhortation to "not treat prophecies with contempt but test them all; hold on to what is good"

(1 Thess. 5:20–21). First, Paul reminds the church to hold its leaders in high regard: “Now we ask you, brothers and sisters, to acknowledge those who work hard among you, who care for you in the Lord and who admonish you. Hold them in the highest regard in love because of their work” (vv. 12–13a).

One way we can honor church leaders is, if possible, to tell them the gist of the word before a meeting. Doing so allows them to consider the most appropriate time to share the prophecy during the service.

Second, Paul addresses relationships with each other: “Live in peace with each other. And we urge you, brothers and sisters, warn those who are idle and disruptive, encourage the disheartened, help the weak, be patient with everyone. Make sure that nobody pays back wrong for wrong, but always strive to do what is good for each other and for everyone else” (vv. 13b–15).

Finally, Paul addresses their relationship with God: “Rejoice always, pray continually, give thanks in all circumstances; for this is God’s will for you in Christ Jesus. Do not quench the Spirit” (vv. 16–19).

I am always more cautious when I hear a prophecy from someone with disorderly relationships. We shouldn’t dismiss their insights outright because spiritual gifts are not a sign of maturity but availability. Nonetheless, I want to carefully sift what is said, especially if the prophecy calls for action. If the prophecy is especially significant for a church, we must not rush our prayerful consideration. We do not expect the Supreme Court to rule on an essential matter in ten seconds, nor should church leaders. Say: "Thanks so much for sharing. We want to take time to consider your words prayerfully so that we know how to respond individually and as a church."

A wise pastor I know often asks those new to prophetic ministry if they will allow him to give their prophecy. He wants to find out what's really in the person's heart. If the person is genuinely concerned that the congregation hears the prophetic insight, they never take issue with the pastor sharing the message. However, as is sometimes the case, if the person craves attention and insists on being the one who delivers the insight, then that gives the pastor pause for thought.

Earlier in his letter to the Thessalonians, Paul advises communicating the right way. He doesn't explicitly mention prophetic ministry here, but we can read it as included:

> On the contrary, we speak as those approved by God to be entrusted with the gospel. We are not trying to please people but God, who tests our

> hearts. You know we never used flattery, nor did we put on a mask to cover up greed—God is our witness. We were not looking for praise from people, not from you or anyone else, even though as apostles of Christ we could have asserted our authority. Instead, we were like young children among you. (1 Thess. 2:4–7)

When I listen to prophetic insight, I quickly run through this list:

- Does this person speak as one approved by God?
- Has God entrusted anything to them? Have I found them trustworthy?
- Is the person a people pleaser?
- Is the person prone to flattery? (There's a big gap between wanting to encourage someone and flattering them. Flattery is always manipulative. Encouragement says *I have your best interests at heart*; flattery never loses sight of its own interests.)
- Is this person authentic? Do they wear masks?
- Are they greedy?
- Are they fishing for compliments?
- Are they bossy and insistent?
- Are they gentle in their approach to others?

I've exhibited all these characteristics at different times, good and bad. I'm thankful for grace-filled leaders who took me aside, mentored me, and showed me how to speak tenderly through my prophetic ministry.

Questions for Reflection and Discussion

1. Have you ever thought spiritual gifts were just for super-holy or super-spiritual people? Why do you think God wants all to use spiritual gifts but restricts leadership only to those exhibiting certain character qualities?

2. Imagine you have been asked to paraphrase the Bible to include the people of your city or community. How would you paraphrase Peter's quotation from the prophet Joel: "'In the last days, God says, I will pour out my Spirit on all people. Your sons and daughters will prophesy, your young men will see visions, your old men will dream dreams. Even on my servants, both men and women, I will pour out my Spirit in those days, and they will prophesy'" (Acts 2:17–18)?

3. In Jeremiah 29:7, Jeremiah writes prophetically to God's people in Babylonian exile, instructing them to "seek the

peace and prosperity of the city to which I have carried you into exile. Pray to the LORD for it, because if it prospers, you too will prosper." How might you or your church seek prayer for the peace and prosperity of your city or community?

4. Do you have a system to record and review any insights or prophetic messages you believe the Lord has spoken to you? If so, read back over them. What patterns can you detect? Are there some insights you dismissed at the time but now, in hindsight, seem very relevant? If so, thank God. Are there still insights that seem confusing, troubling, or possibly wrong? Bring them to the Lord and leave them with him. If they are genuine insights from the Lord, he will make that clear in his ways and in his time.

5. Reread 1 Thessalonians 2:4–6. How might your Christian walk and prophetic ministry change if you focus on pleasing God rather than pleasing people? How might your life change if you were not concerned about receiving praise from others?

3

Eagerly Desire Spiritual Gifts, Especially Prophecy

> Follow the way of love and eagerly desire gifts of the Spirit, especially prophecy.
>
> —1 Corinthians 14:1

Can you imagine your Amazon delivery driver's face when, on successive days, eight milking maids, nine dancing ladies, ten jumping noblemen, and eleven members of an orchestra's woodwind section all jump off his truck and head to your front door? The following day the delivery driver is even more bemused when a dozen members of a drumline squeeze into the delivery van with their cymbals, toms, snares, and bass drums!

Your neighbors will be twitching their curtains and pursing their lips if the band begins banging those bad-boy drums before dawn on January 5, the twelfth day of Christmas.

Perhaps you've never given Epiphany much thought. I hadn't until Marta, our Spanish exchange student, told us the most significant Christmas celebration in Spain was on January 6, Three King's Day, the first day of Epiphany.

You are probably familiar with the visit of the Magi from Matthew 2. However, you may have overlooked one small but essential part of the account. Let's read Matthew 2:1–12 together:

> After Jesus was born in Bethlehem in Judea, during the time of King Herod, Magi from the east came to Jerusalem and asked, "Where is the one who has been born King of the Jews? We saw his star when it rose and have come to worship him."
>
> When King Herod heard this he was disturbed, and all Jerusalem with him. When he had called together all the people's chief priests and teachers of the law, he asked them where the Messiah was to be born. "In Bethlehem in Judea," they replied, "for this is what the prophet has written:

> "'But you, Bethlehem, in the land of Judah,
> are by no means least among the rulers
> of Judah;
> for out of you will come a ruler
> who will shepherd my people Israel.'"
>
> Then Herod called the Magi secretly and found out from them the exact time the star had appeared. He sent them to Bethlehem and said, "Go and search carefully for the child. As soon as you find him, report to me, so that I too may go and worship him."
>
> After they had heard the king, they went on their way, and the star they had seen when it rose went ahead of them until it stopped over the place where the child was. When they saw the star, they were overjoyed. On coming to the house, they saw the child with his mother Mary, and they bowed down and worshiped him. Then they opened their treasures and presented him with gifts of gold, frankincense and myrrh. And having been warned in a dream not to go back to Herod, they returned to their country by another route.

Matthew doesn't tell us where the Magi came from other than that they came from *the east*. Some Bible scholars suggest they were Persian Zoroastrian astrologer-philosophers; others favor Yemen as their country of origin, and others postulate India or China. Wherever it was, it was a long enough journey to the City of David that God provided a star to guide them.

Persia is almost 1,000 miles from Bethlehem; Yemen, 1,250 miles; India, 2,500; and China, more than 4,000 miles. At a top camel speed of 100 miles per day, these journeys would have taken ten days, twelve days, twenty-five days, or forty days, respectively. It was a trip the Magi had to plan carefully to ensure they carried sufficient provisions to cross unrelenting terrain to an unknown final destination. It was not a casual trip down the road to the newsagents or grocery store; it was an expedition.

"It's a long journey," I hear you say, "we agree. So what's the point?" Here's the point, these nonbelievers traveled for days to worship King Jesus. In contrast, Herod did not bother to travel 4.8 miles from Jerusalem to Bethlehem to check out the Magi's claims about this newborn king of the Jews. We learn from Scripture that Herod was disturbed, but not enough to walk three hours to investigate the Magi's claims. He could have ridden over to that small walled town, with an estimated population of between three hundred to five hundred, on his lunch hour. If Mary and Joseph had already returned to Nazareth, the distance would have been longer, roughly 91 miles. Still far shorter than the Magi's journey. Herod made neither journey. Herod outsourced the investigation to the Magi, instructing them to bring him a report on their way home.

Tragically, when it comes to the things of the Holy Spirit, many Western Christians, including myself, are sometimes more like Herod than the Magi. We get comfortable. We want everything brought to us. We want the flame of the Holy Spirit but avoid any inconvenient searching for the fire to set our hearts alight.

If we hope to develop a prophetic fire, we must search and study. And, when we get a light, we must continually fan it into flame. We have to build Magi moments into our life.

I remember visiting a church of several hundred people in Belfast, Northern Ireland, in early 1995. I don't remember the worship or the preaching at all. All I remember is that a man several rows in front of me trembled throughout the entire service. His body quivered, rippled, and shook; I'd never seen anything like it. I wasn't sure if he had a neurological condition or was fighting an alcohol addiction cold turkey.

To my surprise, before his sermon, the pastor called this man to the pulpit and asked him to share his recent experience in the Vineyard Church in Toronto, Canada. The man explained that he had heard reports of God pouring out his Spirit in the Canadian church; he was hungry and thirsty and wanted to be refreshed by the Spirit. I'm sure his visit was costly. Likely, he had to use his annual vacation leave and pay several thousand dollars for flights and hotel accommodations. I certainly don't advocate that we run after every rumor or report of God at work. However, if we want to experience God's fire, we may have to visit places where the Spirit has chosen to work in powerful ways.

I don't know what happened in that church because of that man's visit. I know many who visited the Toronto Vineyard Church brought back great refreshments to their home churches. What impressed me is that he went to investigate and had a powerful encounter with the Spirit. Unlike James Bond's vodka martini, this man was *shaken and stirred.*

To catch prophetic fire, we must search, study, and settle on what the Scriptures tell us.

Boiling Point

Kathie always reminds me of Paul's words to stir up my gifting. In his letter to the Corinthian church, the apostle Paul instructs members of this fledgling Gentile church:

"Follow the way of love and eagerly desire gifts of the Spirit, especially prophecy" (1 Cor. 14:1).

This English translation, "follow," doesn't adequately capture the Greek word *diōkete*, which conveys the idea of a hunter chasing down its prey. There is no casualness in Paul's exhortation here. *Diōkete* is the word most often used in the context of persecution. Jesus uses a word from the same root, *diōkeis*, when he interrupts Saul on the road to Damascus, saying, "I am Jesus, whom you are persecuting" (Acts 9:5). Paul didn't casually follow Christians to put them in prison. He "began to destroy the church. Going from house to house, he dragged off both men and women and put them in prison" (8:3). Paul tells us to pursue agape love with this intensity, passion, and rigor.

After his exposition on agape love in 1 Corinthians 13, Paul might have continued his treatise in numerous ways. He might have written: Follow the way of love and show hospitality to one another. Follow the way of love and encourage one another daily. Follow the way of love, and don't forget to keep meeting together.

All of these would have been good things to say. But Paul didn't emphasize these here. Instead, he implies that if we're seriously going to chase love down, we need to eagerly desire the Holy Spirit's gifts.

The English translation, “eagerly desire” (14:1), doesn’t capture the nuances of the Greek word *zēlout* either. The word is onomatopoeic and sounds like water on the boil. Water needs intense heat to reach its boiling point. Paul asks us to burn with that force of zealous energy seeking spiritual gifts.

Paul identifies prophecy as the gift that best enables us to pursue agape. Why? Because prophecy encourages, strengthens, and comforts (v. 3). It reveals the heart’s secrets (v. 25). It edifies the church (v. 4). No wonder Paul concludes this section of his letter by telling the church to *zēloute to prophesy.*

Strengthen, Encourage, and Comfort

Paul’s encouragement to eagerly desire to prophesy does not give us the license to prophesy irresponsibly. Nowadays, whenever I teach people new to prophetic ministry, I encourage them to seek words to strengthen, encourage, and comfort. If you have ever seen children learn how to bowl at the local bowling alley, you may have noticed their parents helping them in three ways:

1. The mom or dad ensures the child selects a ball that is not too heavy for them;

2. The parent will help the child roll their bowling ball down a ramp so that it gathers enough momentum to reach the pins; and
3. Parents will pull up the bumpers on each side of the lane to prevent the child's ball from rolling into the gulley.

Even a beginner is likely to hit the pins if parents do these things. Paul's admonition to prophesy to strengthen, encourage, and comfort is the prophetic equivalent of bowling alley bumpers. If you focus on these, you'll likely hit some pins and, equally important, won't do much harm.

I haven't always followed my advice. I remember leading a small group in my living room several years ago. During one group meeting, I sensed the Lord had a prophetic word for one of the young women present that evening. Sometimes when I prophesy, the Lord gives me a picture as a launching point. Sometimes it's some words or a phrase. Sometimes I know the Lord has something to communicate to this person, and I have to speak out in faith, confident the words will come. On these occasions, it's very much an "open wide your mouth and I will fill it" type of invitation (Ps. 81:10). That was the case when I prophesied over Sarah.

Sarah was in her late teens or early twenties with shoulder-length, dark-brown hair. She had beautiful Irish eyes, but they always looked sad. As I began to prophesy over Sarah, I heard myself say, "The Lord has a husband for you." I've taught about using prophetic gifts responsibly in many countries. I have always counseled people to be very cautious about prophesying about marriage. It's not that God is not interested in marriage. He certainly is. But I also know how easy it is for people to confuse their desires for an unmarried friend to find a partner with the voice of the Lord. When we want something good for a friend, we must be careful not to confuse our emotions with an insight from the Holy Spirit. I couldn't believe I had told this young woman, "God has a husband for you." I knew a little about Sarah's background. She had been raped multiple times by a close family member. When she eventually told her mom, her mom would not believe her. The abuse continued for several years until Sarah moved to Dublin.

Sarah always wore baggy clothes to hide her femininity. She hated men. The last thing she wanted to do was get married. As soon as I prophesied those words about marriage, Sarah burst into tears and ran out of the room. I felt stupid and ashamed. Here I was, an elder in the church, breaking my own rules and deeply wounding a vulnerable young woman in our group. I continued to lead the group while Kathie slipped out of the room and followed Sarah upstairs. I can't remember what I told the group, but I clearly remember what was going through my mind. *Stupid, stupid, stupid,* I told myself. I felt dreadful. I desperately wanted to unsay those words. But God had other ideas.

Sarah was married a year later to a wonderful man.

I spoke with Sarah about the incident. She told me that she had built a thick, self-protective wall around her heart after her abuse. She'd been hurt enough and didn't want anyone to hurt her again. The trouble with any emotional barriers we build up is that they keep both good and bad out just as effectively as they keep both good and bad locked up inside. Sarah's wall kept all her hurt, anger, shame, self-hatred, and rejection bottled up inside. When I prophesied, "The Lord has a husband for you," the words broke through her protective shell, and the Holy Spirit began to heal her gently from the inside out.

I certainly don't want to minimize Sarah's healing process over the next year before she was ready to marry her husband. There were lots of tears and beautiful moments of healing. But the process started with a prophetic word that I wish I could have taken back, but I am now delighted I could not.

Prophetic words can have the power to destroy strongholds, expose the lies we tell ourselves, and propel us into our destiny. I doubt anyone who knew Sarah then could have imagined her marrying. I certainly could not. But God sees beyond what we can see. He sees possibilities we can't even imagine and can use the prophetic to propel us into a destiny we thought impossible. If you've built up a rigid wall of self-protection, God's word can break it. He did in Sarah's case.

While God redeemed this situation, it might have ended up badly. Paul reminds us that "the spirits of prophets are subject to the control of prophets" (1 Cor. 14:32). This means that even though I was prophesying under the anointing of the Spirit, trusting the Lord to give me the right words for Sarah, I was still in control of my words. Prophecy is never automatic speech; we are accountable for the words we use in prophecy as much as those we use on the street corner.

Grace and Faith

While this prophetic encounter with Sarah ended well, this is not always the case. Inexperienced, unwise, and, sadly, even manipulative people have prophesied and hurt many people. Like young athletes imitate Simone Biles, Tom

Brady, or Michael Jordan, prophetic ministers often emulate those with significant giftings. While we can certainly learn from those with different giftings, we need to be careful not to operate beyond our level of grace and faith.

Paul gives us some helpful instructions in Romans 12:6. Here, he reminds his readers that: "We have different gifts, according to the grace given to each of us. If your gift is prophesying, then prophesy in accordance with your faith."

Paul identifies two important limiters on our prophetic ministry: the type of grace-gifts given to us and our level of faith. Those maturing in prophetic ministry find their grace-gifts differ in how the Holy Spirit streams insight to them and the spheres of influence in which they can effectively operate.

Before considering common ways that the Holy Spirit livestreams insights in prophetic ministry, I want to emphasize that most of these are simple thoughts and mental pictures. In most cases, this is all that the Holy Spirit needs to communicate to do his work powerfully. We must never look down on these and think they are less spiritual than visions or audible voices. From time to time, the Holy Spirit might choose to livestream prophetic insights in more unusual ways. There are several, but the most common are bubbling up, hearing, and seeing.

Bubbling Up: People sometimes experience a prophetic flow rather than a singular prophetic insight. It's as if prophetic insights bubble up from within them. In John 7:38–39, Jesus tells his listeners that the living waters of the Spirit will flow from those who believe in him. When we believe, we often discover that prophetic insights flow in the Spirit's stream. I experience this *bubbling up* of prophetic insight most often during ministry times.

Hearing: Others receive prophetic insight through hearing the Spirit's voice audibly or in their heads. In John 12:28, Jesus heard an audible voice from heaven saying, "I have glorified [Jesus's name], and will glorify it again." However, in verse 29, we learn that those without this gift thought they had heard only thunder.

Seeing: This is the ability to see dreams and visions. We see this gift in operation in 2 Kings 6:15–17. If you recall the scripture, you'll know that the Aramean army surrounded Elijah and his servant. When Elijah's servant saw the Arameans surrounding them, he panicked:

> "Oh no, my lord! What shall we do?" the servant asked.
>
> "Don't be afraid," the prophet answered. "Those who are with us are more than those who are with them."

> And Elisha prayed, "Open his eyes, LORD, so that he may see." Then the LORD opened the servant's eyes, and he looked and saw the hills full of horses and chariots of fire all around Elisha.

When we begin moving in prophetic ministry, we often have a primary means of receiving insight, whether it be bubbling up, hearing, or seeing. As we mature prophetically, the Spirit may expand how we receive prophetic revelation. Asking those already operating in those gifts to pray for us is often helpful. The Lord, after all, answered Elijah's prayer and his servant began to see spiritual realities previously hidden from him.

In addition to receiving prophetic insights differently, prophetic ministers have different spheres of influence. God graced Daniel and Joseph with the ability to interpret dreams (Dan. 2:24; Gen. 40). Paul "was caught up to the third heaven. Whether it was in the body or out of the body I do not know" (2 Cor. 12:2). Isaiah prophesied about the coming Messiah (Isa. 43). Elijah, Elisha, and Paul raised people from the dead (1 Kings 17:17–24; 2 Kings 4:18–37; Acts 20:7–12). They ministered within the constraints of the grace given to them, and so must we.

Our level of faith is the second limiter to effective ministry. A prophetic insight full of faith is powerful.

However, nothing much happens when we prophesy beyond our faith level. Without faith, prophetic insight has all the power of an undetonated stick of dynamite. When training people, I often ask whether they believe God will do what they have declared. If they are hesitant, I encourage them to pray, seeking God's spark of faith to light the fuse.

The Ultimate Reward of Prophetic Ministry

Leading prophetically can be challenging. Your motives may be questioned, and your character challenged. Many Christians believe spiritual gifts died out after the apostolic age. Isn't it better to leave controversial gifts aside to maintain Christian unity? Sometimes you pour your heart out to the Lord, seeking insight for a friend or church member, only to have your words dismissed. If we add to this the fact that you will sometimes mishear or misspeak, you might well ask yourself, *Why bother to lead prophetically at all?* Moses has some good answers.

I learned much about leadership from Moses. God gives Moses an unusual sign when he calls Moses to lead God's people out of Egypt. Let's read God's invitation and prophetic sign together from Exodus 3:12: "And God said, 'I will be with you. And this will be the sign to you that it is I who have sent you: When you have brought the people out of Egypt, you will worship God on this mountain.'"

English Bible translations don't capture this well, but the pronoun "you" changes from singular to plural in the sentence. It more accurately reads: "When you [singular] have brought the people out of Egypt, you [plural] will worship God on this mountain."

I wonder what must have gone through Moses's mind. Perhaps it was something like this:

> Okay, so here I am standing on Mount Horeb, and you want me to go back to Egypt, where I might still be wanted for murder. I'm to go to Pharoah, who probably thinks I deserve to die. If Pharoah doesn't kill me, which he probably will, you want me to speak to the Hebrews. They wanted nothing to do with me forty years ago. But now you want me to tell them that their God, the God of Abraham, Isaac, and Jacob, sent me to lead them out of captivity. And if the Hebrews don't kill me, my reward, my sign, is that I'll get to return to the very rock I'm standing on right now, and we can all worship together. Perhaps you hadn't noticed, but I'm standing here already. I don't have to do any of that to be here with you. As offers go, that's underwhelming! What's in it for me?

Moses tries every which way to avoid taking on this call to lead. He asks for more signs, and God shows him some neat tricks with snakes and a now-you-see-it-now-you-don't leprous hand. Try as he might, Moses couldn't wiggle out of this responsibility and heads off for his first appointment with Pharoah.

Let's fast-forward over ten plagues, a miraculous sea crossing, and a ton of sand. Moses eventually does return to the very spot where God called him to lead. In Exodus 19, we read that God gives a tremendous promise to Moses and the people when they arrive at Mount Sinai, another name for Mount Horeb: "'Now if you obey me fully and keep my covenant, then out of all nations you will be my treasured possession. Although the whole earth is mine, you will be for me a kingdom of priests and a holy nation.' These are the words you are to speak to the Israelites" (vv. 5–6).

Now that's a better reward! *A treasured possession.*

However, it doesn't take the Israelites long to break their side of the covenant. Soon after, God calls Moses up to the summit of Mount Sinai for a lengthy chat. He returns to base camp slower than the Israelites expected. They get restless. Let's pick up the story in Exodus 32:1: "When the people saw that Moses was so long in coming down from the mountain, they gathered around Aaron and said, 'Come, make us gods who will go before us. As for this fellow Moses who brought us up out of Egypt, we don't know what has happened to him.'"

God's prophetic sign to Moses, recorded in Exodus 3:12, was: "When you [singular] have brought the people out of Egypt, you [plural] will worship God on this mountain." However, instead of worshipping God, the Israelites worshipped an idol. Moses's heart must have been broken. God's heart certainly was. Let's read on into the first few verses of Exodus 33:

> Then the Lord said to Moses, "Leave this place, you and the people you brought up out of Egypt, and go up to the land I promised on oath to Abraham, Isaac and Jacob, saying, 'I will give it to your descendants.' I will send an angel before you and drive out the Canaanites, Amorites, Hittites, Perizzites, Hivites and Jebusites. Go up to the land flowing with milk and honey. But I will not go with you, because you are a stiff-necked people and I might destroy you on the way." (vv. 1–3)

When God calls Moses in Exodus 3:12, he tells Moses, "I will be with you." At this stage in Moses's leadership journey, he did not think God's presence was enough. Moses wanted signs and wonders. However, by Exodus 33:1–3, something remarkable has happened in Moses's heart. God has just told Moses that he will still give the Israelites the land promised to Abraham, Isaac, and Jacob. God tells Moses that he will "send an angel before you and drive out the Canaanites, Amorites, Hittites, Perizzites, Hivites, and Jebusites." God promises Moses a land "flowing with milk and honey." Now that seems a proper reward for all those years of hardship. But then God tells Moses "I will not go with you."

Moses responds: "If your Presence does not go with us, do not send us up from here. How will anyone know that you are pleased with me and with your people unless you go with us? What else will distinguish me and your people from all the other people on the face of the earth?" (vv. 15–16).

In Exodus 3, Moses didn't think God's presence was enough. He wanted signs and wonders. By Exodus 33, a significant leadership reversal has happened in Moses's heart. Now signs and wonders are not enough. What Moses longs for is God's presence. If you are a leader, allow this word to sink deeply into your weary soul. Your reward for leading is knowing God more intimately and enjoying his presence in new and profound ways. And when you know God intimately and carry his presence, you'll have opportunities for ministry seasoned with grace.

Questions for Reflection and Discussion

1. On a scale of 1–10, how eagerly do you desire spiritual gifts, especially the gift of prophecy? Have you reached the boiling point in your search? If not, how could you intensify the flame?

2. Why do you think Paul tells us to follow the way of love before we pursue spiritual gifts? What might happen if we don't follow this advice?

3. Have you ever been at a meeting where you experienced an outpouring of the Holy Spirit? If so, what happened? How did this experience impact you at the time? Has anything changed since?

4. Seedbed exists as a resource for the people of God for a great awakening. How might developing mature prophetic ministry help?

5. God is, by very nature, ever-present. There is no place he does not inhabit in the universe. Psalm 139 reminds us that we cannot flee from his presence. Yet, Psalm 95 instructs us to enter his presence with thanksgiving. What do you think it means to enter his presence?

Questions for Reflection and Discussion

4

Creative Prophecy

> Seek the Lord while he may be found;
> call on him while he is near.
>
> —Isaiah 55:6

In Jeremiah 18, we read how God instructed Jeremiah to go to the potter's house. Jeremiah knew God would speak to him there, but he had no idea what God would say. Let's read the passage together to see how the story unfolds. We'll begin with Jeremiah 18:1–4:

> This is the word that came to Jeremiah from the Lord: "Go down to the potter's house, and there I will give you my message." So I went down to the potter's house, and I saw him working at the

> wheel. But the pot he was shaping from the clay was marred in his hands; so the potter formed it into another pot, shaping it as seemed best to him.

When Jeremiah arrives, he has a good look around. He sees the potter working at his wheel, but the pot he is making goes all wonky, and he must start all over again. I've thrown only two pots in my life, and had the same experience as Jeremiah's potter both times: my pots didn't turn out as I had hoped, and I had to start all over again. It's a common, everyday experience for a potter.

God only spoke after Jeremiah had paid attention to the potter at work. Let's read verses 5–10 to see how God uses the potter's work to illustrate his intentions:

> Then the word of the LORD came to me. He said, "Can I not do with you, Israel, as this potter does?" declares the LORD. "Like clay in the hand of the potter, so are you in my hand, Israel. If at any time I announce that a nation or kingdom is to be uprooted, torn down and destroyed, and if that nation I warned repents of its evil, then I will relent and not inflict on it the disaster I had planned. And if at another time I announce that a nation or kingdom is to be built up and planted, and if it does evil in my sight and does not obey

> me, then I will reconsider the good I had intended to do for it.

The final section, verses 11–12, is a call to action:

> "Now therefore say to the people of Judah and those living in Jerusalem, 'This is what the Lord says: Look! I am preparing a disaster for you and devising a plan against you. So turn from your evil ways, each one of you, and reform your ways and your actions.' But they will reply, 'It's no use. We will continue with our own plans; we will all follow the stubbornness of our evil hearts.'"

The prophecy illustrates a typical three-step process in prophetic ministry. First, God shows us an object or prophetic picture. Next, he explains how what we see relates to something in his heart. Finally, he gives us a call to action, letting us know how he wants us to respond to the insight. What's also interesting is that God uses everyday things to speak to Jeremiah. God speaks to Jeremiah where he is and will do the same for you and me.

It's easy for us to reduce prophetic ministry to spoken words. Words are important. But we must recognize God's creativity in prophetic ministry. God could have spoken the same message to Jeremiah in his bedroom, the marketplace, or the temple. Instead, God asked Jeremiah to walk down the road to visit the pottery and watch the potter working at his wheel. It's as if God wants to underline his message visually. It's a powerful tool. Many of us can recall what God said through Jeremiah only because we connect it with the potter's work. God's a communication genius.

Scripture is crammed with prophetic acts. For example, God tells Ezekiel to pack his bags symbolically:

> "Therefore, son of man, pack your belongings for exile and in the daytime, as they watch, set out and go from where you are to another place. Perhaps they will understand, though they are a rebellious people. During the daytime, while they watch, bring out your belongings packed for exile. Then in the evening, while they are watching, go out like those who go into exile. While they watch, dig through the wall and take your belongings out through it. Put them on your shoulder as they are watching and carry them out at dusk. Cover your face so that you cannot see the land, for I have made you a sign to the Israelites." (Ezek. 12:3–6)

There are many more. Here are just a few: Ezekiel prophetically groans (21:6), marks out two roads and puts up a signpost (vv. 18–23), and writes on a couple of sticks (37:15–17); Elijah throws his mantle on Elisha (1 Kings 19:19–21); Moses lifts a bronze serpent on a pole (Num. 21:8); Elisha shoots an arrow (2 Kings 13:14–19); Agabus binds Paul's hands with his belt (Acts 21:10–11); Zechariah makes a silver and gold crown (Zech. 6:9–12); and Isaiah walks around partially naked (Isa. 20:2).

We could add all the varieties of prophetic dreams and visions to this list. Additionally, we must not overlook that God filled artisans with his Spirit to enhance their creative work. Exodus 31:1–5 tells us about Bezalel:

> Then the LORD said to Moses, "See, I have chosen Bezalel son of Uri, the son of Hur, of the tribe of Judah, and I have filled him with the Spirit of God, with wisdom, with understanding, with knowledge and with all kinds of skills—to make artistic designs for work in gold, silver and bronze, to cut and set stones, to work in wood, and to engage in all kinds of crafts."

Why would craftsmen need to be filled with the Spirit? Why didn't God instruct Moses to hire the best artisans available? God didn't choose to fill Bezalel with his Spirit to make him a better craftsman; God did it to help Bezalel faithfully communicate the wonder of God's heart for his people. Before Pentecost, other than prophets, priests, and kings, few were filled with the Holy Spirit. Bezalel was one. Elizabeth, John the Baptist's mom, was another. Both infillings resulted in prophecy.

Bezalel proclaims the majesty and glory of God through his artistic designs using precious metals, stones, and wood. In Luke 1:42–45, we read that when Elizabeth was filled with the Holy Spirit she prophesied over her relative Mary, shouting with a loud voice:

> "Blessed are you among women, and blessed is the child you will bear! But why am I so favored, that the mother of my Lord should come to me? As soon as the sound of your greeting reached my ears, the baby in my womb leaped for joy. Blessed is she who has believed that the Lord would fulfill his promises to her!"

God speaks in many ways through artists, designers, and architects, just as he speaks through the prophetic shout of an older woman entering her third trimester of pregnancy.

Prophetic Ministry 101

It is challenging to mature prophetically until we first learn how the Holy Spirit speaks to us individually. The more we have learned to discern the Holy Spirit's voice and presence accurately and regularly, the easier it will be for us to spot his prophetic livestreams. Even after following Jesus for forty-plus years, I am still learning. But I am now far more able to tune into the Spirit than I was when I first became a Jesus-follower.

Early in my followership of Jesus, the Lord impressed on me a verse from the book of Isaiah: Isaiah 55:6:

> Seek the LORD while he may be found;
> call on him while he is near.

The more I meditated on this verse, the more I sensed that the Lord was telling me to pay attention when he came close. Of course, God, by his very nature, is everywhere. Yet, there are times when he more clearly discloses his presence, and the Lord instructed me to pay particular attention during these times. I wanted to seek the Lord and call on him when he was near.

Part of my seeking was through my study of Scripture. As I read the Bible, chapter after chapter, book after book, I spotted many things I had previously missed. For example, I noticed how biblical characters experienced the Holy Spirit's presence. I saw that Samuel initially couldn't distinguish God's voice from his mentor, Eli's. To Samuel, God's voice must have sounded so ordinary (1 Sam. 3). To

Elijah, God's voice was still and small (1 Kings 19:11–13). To the apostle John, God's voice sounded like mighty rushing waters, deafeningly loud (Rev. 1:15).

When Saul met a group of prophets in 1 Samuel 10:10, the Scripture tells us that "the Spirit of God came powerfully upon him, and he joined in their prophesying." I wondered how the Spirit mightily coming on him felt. Jeremiah experienced joy when God's word came to him (Jer. 15:16). Adam heard the Lord walking in the garden (Gen. 3:8). How, I wondered, would that have sounded? I doubted it sounded like feet kicking rustling leaves, but I could not guess what Adam might have heard. John fell at Jesus's feet "as though dead" (Rev. 1:17). I pondered how that may have felt. David experienced God's heavy hand on him (Ps. 32:4), Isaiah experienced God's calling and anointing like a burning coal (Isa. 6:6–7), the psalmist trembled in God's presence (Ps. 119:120), and all Daniel's strength left him after he saw a vision (Dan. 10:8). I could go on, but you get the point: people responded in very different ways to the presence of the Holy Spirit, and I wanted to learn how the Lord might reveal himself to me.

The more I read about how individuals responded to the presence of the Holy Spirit, the more curious I became. I began to note how God trained people in prophetic ministry. It was intriguing that the Lord often taught prophets by asking them questions. Jeremiah 1:11–15a illustrates this:

> The word of the Lord came to me: "What do you see, Jeremiah?"
>
> "I see the branch of an almond tree," I replied.
>
> The Lord said to me, "You have seen correctly, for I am watching to see that my word is fulfilled."
>
> The word of the Lord came to me again: "What do you see?"
>
> "I see a pot that is boiling," I answered. "It is tilting toward us from the north."
>
> The Lord said to me, "From the north disaster will be poured out on all who live in the land. I am about to summon all the peoples of the northern kingdoms," declares the Lord.

This encounter is fascinating for all sorts of reasons. It's as if Jeremiah is in Prophetic Ministry 101. I imagine his classes may have gone something like this:

GOD:	Welcome to Prophetic Ministry 101, Jeremiah. You can sit there.
JEREMIAH:	Am I the only one in class?
GOD:	Yes, all my classes are one-to-one.

JEREMIAH: Okay. That's a little overwhelming, but I'll get used to it.

GOD: Let's get started. Jeremiah, tell me, what do you see?

JEREMIAH: Uh, I see an almond tree.

GOD: Bull's-eye. Well done, Jeremiah. That's right. You're off to a great start. Did you notice the word I used for almond, *šā·qêḏ*, also means "watched"? I sometimes use wordplay in prophetic messages.

JEREMIAH: Why do you do that?

GOD: Have a guess?

JEREMIAH: To help people to remember your words?

GOD: Yes, exactly. Now, whenever you see an almond tree, you'll remember I'm watching over my word to perform it.

JEREMIAH: Ah, now I see. Do you use wordplay a lot?

GOD: Yes, I often use it. Did you read the first chapter of the prophet Micah as part of your prereading? I enjoyed working with him one hundred years ago.

JEREMIAH: Yes, I read Micah.

GOD: Did you see how I incorporated the meaning of each town's name in the prophecy I gave to each place?

JEREMIAH: Uh, no, I must have missed that. Can you explain?

GOD: Let me read some of the lines from Micah 1:10–15:

> Tell it not in Gath
> weep not at all. (v. 10a)

Did you know *Gath* sounds like the Hebrew for "tell"? That was some fun wordplay.

> In Beth Ophrah
> roll in the dust. (v. 10b)

Ophrah means "House of Dust."

> Those who live in Zaanan
> will not come out. (v. 11b)

Zaanan sounds like the Hebrew for "come out."

> Those who live in Maroth writhe in pain . . . (v. 12a)

Maroth sounds like the Hebrew for "bitter."

> The town of Akzib will prove deceptive
> to the kings of Israel. (v. 14b)

Akzib means "deception."

> I will bring a conqueror against you
> who live in Mareshah. (v. 15a)

Did you realize *Mareshah* sounds like the Hebrew for "conqueror"?

Do you see how I incorporated each town's name to help the residents remember my judgment? It helps them to remember what's coming unless they get back on track with me. Come back tomorrow. I have another lesson to teach you.

The Next Day . . .

GOD: Welcome to Prophetic Ministry 102. Let's get started straightaway. Jeremiah, what do you see?

JEREMIAH: That's easy. I see a boiling pot.

GOD: Look more closely. You've missed an important detail.

JEREMIAH: The pot is tilting this way.

GOD: Yes, from which direction?

JEREMIAH: How can I know that?

GOD: Look at the positioning of the sun. Think about it.

JEREMIAH: Oh yes! Now I see. The sun always rises in the east, so that must be north.

GOD: Now, put all those pieces together. What do you see?

JEREMIAH: I see a pot that is boiling and is tipping toward us from the north.

GOD: That's correct. Jeremiah, ensure you pay attention to those little details as they may be essential. I showed you the pot tipping from the north to remind you that I will use all the northern kingdoms to help get my people back on track.

We don't know from Scripture whether Jeremiah saw a real almond tree and a boiling pot or whether they were visions. The Lord uses both. In Isaiah 6, the prophet sees a vision of the Lord filling the temple with glory. In Jeremiah 18:2, the Lord tells Jeremiah: "Go down to the potter's house, and there I will give you my message." If you are familiar with the passage, you'll know that the Lord spoke to Jeremiah using the potter working at his wheel as a focal point of the prophetic message. Visions are not more spiritual than natural objects. God uses both. He might easily have given Jeremiah a vision of a potter at work, but for reasons we do not know chose not to.

Action Man

If God uses everyday objects to help his people remember what he is saying, so can we. Some twenty years ago or so, St. Mark's Church in Dublin, Ireland, invited me to lead an evening of prophetic ministry. I took a sack of children's toys with me and incorporated a toy in every prophecy to help the person remember what was said. For example, at one point in the evening, I dug into my sack and pulled out an Action Man (the UK version of G.I. Joe). Years later, one young man, Des, still remembers what I said:

> You called me up and had an Action Man doll in your hand. I was in good shape then, and you joked that the Action Man didn't represent me

physically, but that God would use me to instigate "action." I would hear His voice and be someone that would "act" on what I felt He was saying. You referenced Joshua in your prophecy, saying I would lead people into God's promises. There would be significant obstacles (the river Jordan and the fortified cities), but I was not to be afraid. I was to keep my eyes on Jesus; He would lead and strengthen me to lead others.

Judith and I sometimes joke that it's your fault we got so heavily involved in missions and ministry within our church. Since your prophecy, I've worked with Teen Challenge, led the St. Mark's Youth Ministry, co-led St. Mark's Church with Pastor Sean Mullarkey, and planted St. Mark's South with Judith. The church has planted several churches: St. Mark's South, St. Mark's Rescue church, St. Mark's D24, and St. Mark's Balbriggan. We have a St. Mark's church in the Philippines and Poland. We support 100 children and their families in Togo through compassion and have supported churches there and built wells.

I know we joke about it being your fault, but I'm grateful that God used you to speak into my life over 20+ years ago.

Pandora Bracelet

One joy of prophetic ministry is marveling at the creative ways God communicates his love to individuals. My interaction with Kristen is a good example. My wife, Kathie, and Kristen were good friends, but I didn't know her well. She was a talented worship leader in her early thirties who wanted to get married but had not met the right man.

Kristen's father died when she was only twelve. Besides a brother living thousands of miles away, to my knowledge, she had only a few older married men from whom she could seek advice. One morning at church, I kept having the oddest thought. It was simply this: I needed to "adopt" Kristen as my daughter until she was married. My initial response was to reject the idea. It sounded creepy to me, a fifty-year-old guy asking to be a father figure for a thirty-year-old woman. Yet, the thought persisted over the next few days.

What should I do? How could I test this thought? What would you have done?

I did what I encourage every married man to do: I asked my wife! Kathie has excellent discernment and great wisdom. She knew me well and knew Kristen far better than I knew her.

"I keep having this thought about Kristen," I told her one day over lunch.

"Go on," she said.

"The other day in church, I had this compelling thought that I should offer to be a father to Kristen until she gets married."

"She's not even dating."

"I realize that. This could be a long-term commitment. What do you think?"

"I think you should at least ask her."

When Kathie and I next met Kristen, I told Kristen I had something to ask her.

We sat down together. I'd rehearsed what I wanted to say, but I hadn't anticipated that asking Kristen would be so emotional. I told her about this compelling thought. I told her I could not replace her birth father, whom I knew she loved so deeply. I told her I didn't want anything in return; I just wanted to serve her this way until she married. Then, I burst into tears. It was a holy moment for me.

Kristen said yes to my offer. Being a stand-in father for her, even for a short while, was a tremendous privilege. I helped her financially, prayed for her daily, and met with her every few weeks to ask the questions dads typically ask their daughters. "How's work? How are you doing? How are you doing financially? How's your spiritual life? Met anyone interesting you might want Kathie and me to meet?"

A couple of years later, the Lord gave me another insight for Kristen. I had the strong impression that I should buy a Pandora bracelet for her, buy three stones to place on the bracelet, and tell her that her husband would buy the fourth one. Again, I shared this with Kathie. Once again, she encouraged me to follow through on this impression. So, we went shopping together at a local Pandora jewelry store. We bought a beautiful bracelet, and Kathie helped me pick the charms.

"This one," she told me, "will go well with Kristen's hair color."

"How about this one?" she asked, pointing out one of the more expensive beads.

Half an hour later, we made our final decisions and purchased the bracelet and three charms. The shop assistant wrapped them beautifully, topping the packet with a delicate ribbon bow.

A week or so later, we invited Kristen over for supper. I gave her the small package and told her the prophetic insight I believed the Lord had given me. She opened the box. Her face lit up.

We then prayed for Kristen and told her to pray for her husband whenever she wore the bracelet. We also reminded her that her husband would be the person who would buy her the next charm.

Often, I'd come back from an event Kristen attended, and Kathie would ask me, "Did you see Kristen was wearing your bracelet again tonight?" When we gave the bracelet to Kristen, she was not dating, and there didn't seem to be anyone even on the distant horizon. But Kristen prayed, Kathie and I prayed, and eighteen months later, she met Kory. It was quickly apparent that they were well-suited and watching their romance grow was great fun. They are now married with two beautiful daughters. In case you're wondering, Kory bought her the fourth Pandora charm on their honeymoon.

In this story, we see two prophetic acts. The first was when God asked me to be a surrogate father to Kristen until she met her husband. The second was giving her the Pandora bracelet and three charms, telling her that her husband would buy her the fourth. It was pure joy to be prophetically involved in their coming together and marvel at the goodness of God's plans for them.

Questions for Reflection and Discussion

1. If God can speak in the potter's house, he can speak in your house too. Look around your room, pick one object, and imagine how God might speak to you using that object as a metaphor.

2. Next time you visit a store selling children's toys, walk down the toy aisles and see the variety of toys for sale. Ask God to speak to you using one of the toys you see as a visual aid. God might speak to you there and then, or a thought might bubble up over the coming days. Write down what you sense God is saying to you and incorporate those insights into your prayers.

3. Why do you think God wanted us to know he filled Bezalel, a craftsman, with his Spirit? How might this knowledge change how you think about your career or calling?

4. When he heard Mary's voice, John the Baptist "leaped for joy" in his mother's womb (Luke 1:44). Do you think Elizabeth's phrase is a poetic way of saying John was kicking in her womb, or might it mean John was sensitive to God's presence even while he was being "knit" together in his mother's womb (Ps. 139:13)? Do you think that even unborn children can sense God's presence?

5. What does "Seek the Lord while he may be found" (Isa 55:6a) mean? How are you seeking him?

5

Tuning into the Spirit: Some Activation Exercises

> This is the word that came to Jeremiah from the Lord: "Go down to the potter's house, and there I will give you my message."
>
> —Jeremiah 18:1–2

There's a well-known joke about a person asking for directions. I've heard it about an Englishman asking for directions in Ireland, an Irishman asking for advice in Scotland, a Frenchwoman asking for directions in England, and a tourist asking for directions in New York. I imagine it's told just about everywhere. Here's my version:

A backpacker is walking down a winding country road. She's been walking for ages; her legs are tired, her feet ache, and her backpack seems to weigh more with each step. She's wondering whether she took a wrong turn or if the old map given to her by a friend needs to be updated; it certainly bears no resemblance to the landscape she sees around her. All she knows is that she's completely lost. She keeps plodding along, hoping to see a signpost or meet someone who can give her directions.

An hour later, she hears a distant rumble. She turns around. In the distance, she sees a farm tractor slowly trundling up the road behind her. As it gets nearer, she can see the driver is an older man, wearing a flatcap and wiggling a stick of straw between his teeth. As the tractor nears, the backpacker shouts to the driver for directions to East Farmhampton.

The driver turns off the engine, leans on the steering wheel, and says, "Now, that's better. I couldn't hear a word you said over all that noise. How can I help you?"

Once again, she asks for directions to East Farmhampton.

The tractor driver removes his flatcap, scratches his head, and jiggles the straw from one side of his mouth to the other. After some more thought, he finally replies, "You want to get to East Farmhampton? Well, I wouldn't start from here!"

The joke works better when it's performed rather than read. However, even if you gave the characters great accents and made some excellent tractor engine noises, there are better jokes than this one. But it's a very applicable joke. When I wanted to learn to flow in the Holy Spirit's gifts, I often wished to start somewhere else. I thought I'd learn much faster in a different church, denomination, or location. Even after forty years of ministry, I still feel that way some days. Still, the fact remains, however much we might wish we could start from somewhere else, the only place we can begin is where we are right now. But here's the good news: you have everything you need to start and deepen your prophetic ministry exactly where you are. You can begin by increasing your sensitivity to the Holy Spirit's voice.

Tune-In Exercises

If you have seen an orchestra perform live, you'll have noticed that the orchestra members tune their instruments to the oboe before the conductor enters the stage. The musicians want to ensure their instruments are all in tune with each other before the recital begins. The oboe player plays an A note, and each musician tunes their instrument to that note. It sounds unmelodious, but it is necessary to ensure the performance is not.

Over the years, I've developed three *activation exercises* that help me tune into the Holy Spirit's voice, and I will introduce them in this chapter. Before doing so, discussing God's creativity in prophetic ministry will be helpful. Once you have seen how God often speaks, you'll better grasp how tune-in exercises help me. I hope you find them useful too.

Activation Exercise 1: Everyday Meditations

Let's return to Jeremiah's visit to the potter's house. God could have spoken to Jeremiah anywhere, yet God chose the potter's house to provide a visual aid to his message for Jeremiah. The potter was likely not producing fancy pots for a tourist market, just everyday earthenware for ordinary folk. For all we know, the potter's house might have been at the end of Jeremiah's street. I find this fascinating. If God could use the stuff of everyday life to speak to Jeremiah, then I considered: perhaps he could use the things of my daily life to communicate with me. So I began what I call *everyday meditations*.

In everyday meditations, I tune in by thinking about an ordinary or everyday action or experience, breaking it down into its parts, and meditating on any Scripture verses that come to mind. You can choose any activity: writing a letter, shopping, preparing for a church service, or playing sports. It's not the activity that's important, but the way I prayerfully interact with Scripture that counts.

I'll use kite-flying as an example. In chapter 1, I told the story of my first kite-flying attempts. I have not flown a kite for years, but I have a hunch that if I fly a kite, God will speak to me in and through the experience. If you have a kite, you could join me in this experiment. If not, no worries; you can fly a kite in your imagination. The tune-in exercise will work just as well, but you'll miss the real fun of kite-flying.

I always begin tune-in exercises with prayer: *Holy Spirit, I long for deeper intimacy with you. Please visit me in these moments and over the coming days.* When I began these exercises, I finished my prayer with: *Please speak to me in these moments.* However, I have discovered that the Holy Spirit sometimes bubbles up fresh ideas in the days following and I now look out for them. So, *please speak to me in these moments, and over the coming days,* is how I now pray.

The last time I owned a kite was when my children were small. Back then, I bought a kite at a local toyshop. Nowadays, I have many more choices. Kites vary by size, shape, color, tail length, and the number of strings. All kites are designed to fly but they perform differently in the air.

Some are easy-to-fly diamond or triangular kites. Once these are up in the air, the only control you have over the kite is the length of string you let out as it flies. Stunt kites are more difficult to fly, but if you master the knack, you can do much more with them: you can fly loop-the-loops or complex figure-eight patterns.

I've chosen a bright-green, easy-to-fly beginner kite. I decided based on my budget, interest in kite-flying, and lack of ability.

Here's where the fun begins. I'll ask the Lord to bring scriptures to mind as I engage or think about the activity. I might fly a kite one thousand times, and the scriptures that bubble up might differ every time. If Psalm 139:13–14 bubbles up to remind me how God uniquely designed each of us just as kite manufacturers distinctively create their kites, I'll meditate on these words:

> For you created my inmost being;
> you knit me together in my mother's womb.
> I praise you because I am fearfully and wonderfully made;
> your works are wonderful,
> I know that full well.

Another time I might think about how ridiculous it would be for an easy-to-fly kite to complain that it cannot loop the loop or a stunt kite to complain that it's not so easy for beginners to fly. In the same way, it's not helpful when we compare ourselves to others with different talents. First Corinthians 12:15–18 might come to mind:

> Now if the foot should say, "Because I am not a hand, I do not belong to the body," it would not for that reason stop being part of the body. And if the ear should say, "Because I am not an eye, I do not belong to the body," it would not for that reason stop being part of the body. If the whole body were an eye, where would the sense of hearing be? If the whole body were an ear, where would the sense of smell be? But in fact God has placed the parts in the body, every one of them, just as he wanted them to be.

I think about these differences and begin to thank God that he has made us all differently too. There's plenty to chew on and digest in those verses. A different verse might come to mind. Perhaps Galatians 6:3–5 will bubble up if the Lord wants to set me free from unhealthy comparisons that morning: "If anyone thinks they are something when they are not, they deceive themselves. Each one should test their own actions. Then they can take pride in themselves alone, without comparing themselves to someone else, for each one should carry their own load."

If God wants to remind me that he chose me just as I chose my kite, John 15:16 might come to mind: "You did not choose me, but I chose you and appointed you so that you might go and bear fruit—fruit that will last—and so that whatever you ask in my name the Father will give you."

The beauty of everyday meditations is that I have no idea which verses God might bring to my attention as I reflect on and pray about ordinary, everyday activities. When a verse pops into my mind, I chew on it and then turn it into prayer: *Thank you, Lord, that I didn't choose you; you chose me. Thank you that you chose me to be fruitful. Please help me to produce good fruit. What fruit do you want to grow in and through me this week? What should I be asking you for now? Thank you for wanting me to produce fruit that will last—not fruit kept fresh through preservatives or additives, but fruit kept fresh by your life.*

When my kite is in the air, perhaps God will use the tiny tugs on the line, chasing the kite's tail or the changes in the breeze, to illustrate one point or another. Maybe I'll spot something or someone in my neighborhood for whom the Lord wants me to pray. Perhaps my kite will crash, and the Lord will help me process seasons in my life that did not turn out as I had hoped.

Everyday meditations follow a similar process to an airplane taking off. When I fly, I often look out of the plane's window to see the landscape slope away as the plane takes off. But at other times, I like to sit, close my eyes after the safety demonstration, and see if I can detect the exact moment the aircraft takes off. It's more complicated than you'd think. It's an exciting experience. Often the first movement I notice is moving backward as the pushback tractor pulls the plane back from the gate. Next, I feel the airplane taxiing slowly to the runway. Several stops and starts follow as the plane crawls forward until it is first in line for takeoff. After another pause, the engines roar, and the plane races forward. As it accelerates, you can sometimes feel the wind buffeting the plane or the unevenness of the runway. At some point, the front wheels lift from the ground, then the back wheels, and, finally, you are airborne. The precise moment of takeoff is challenging to detect if you are not looking out of a window, and you may only know you are airborne once the plane begins its steep ascent toward the clouds.

In everyday meditations, my prayerful reflection and scriptural meditation provide the fuel to propel me down the prophetic runway. Sometimes this is all that happens—my wheels, so to speak, never leave the ground. At other times it's as if my front wheels are in the air while my back wheels are still running along the runway. When this happens, I have a mix of thoughts; some are my own, and others might be livestreams from the Holy Spirit—I'm not quite sure. However, sometimes I get up into the air. I'm receptive and focused when this happens, swept along by a prophetic jet stream. Here, it's easy for the Lord to bubble up prophetic insight, often from Scripture, or I see prophetic pictures and visions more clearly than when I am on the ground.

Prophetic insight can come at any time during these meditations. For example, I go for a walk most mornings. I'll pop in my earbuds, find some music, and bop down the street, meditating on Scripture or some recent experience. I might pray about the issues that concern me or spend time preparing for future events. On a morning walk in 2021, I was preparing for my breakout session talk for the New Room Conference in Nashville. I imagined how the breakout room might look, who might register, and how I might pray for people during ministry time. At some point during my walking meditation, I saw a mental picture I thought might be a word of knowledge for someone attending the breakout. I saw a woman looking in a shop window at a knee-length yellow coat. I knew she wanted a coat like this or already had one in her wardrobe. I had yet to learn who this picture was for or how it might be meaningful. I was half-hoping someone would turn up to the breakout session wearing a bright-yellow knee-length coat, but this was unlikely in Nashville's late-summer heat!

During my breakout session, I took the risk of sharing the impression. I said: "I keep seeing a picture of a woman looking through a shop window at a yellow coat. It's a knee-length coat. It's bright yellow. I have no idea how or why this is significant, but a woman here either has or wants a yellow coat. If that's you, I'd like to pray with you."

During our ministry time, a woman approached me and told me she was the woman with a yellow coat.

"How is the coat significant to you?" I asked.

"Every time I consider wearing this coat, I think to myself, *Who are you that you think you can walk around in a coat like this? You're not good enough to wear a bright-yellow coat like that.*"

Clearly, her perception of herself was the issue, not the yellow coat per se. I had an opportunity to minister God's love and goodness to this lady. I hope she now wears that bright-yellow garment with joy and freedom!

Activation Exercise 2: Imaginary Conversations

I remember friends coming to my home when I was a kid, asking, "Is Ivan coming out to play?" They wanted to hang out and be together, with no agenda other than friendship. Likely, someone asked you too. It's a common question. It's an invitation to have fun, forge friendships in make-believe worlds, and get on board the adventure bus of life.

God is much the same. He's always at our doors looking for unlikely people to join him in his work. He's still knocking. But it's not the knock we need to listen for; it's his voice. We sometimes miss his knock, but a voice speaking on the other side of a heavy door is even harder to hear. If we are not paying attention, we hear only the rumble of traffic and the whine of overhead aircraft. However, he promises to come in when we respond to his voice.

Religious art depicts the scene well. I bet you can see some pictures in your mind's eye: Jesus at the door, about to knock. The door handle is on the inside, and only you can open it. I love the imagery, but it misses the most crucial part of this scripture. It is what Jesus wants to come in and do that matters most. Why does Jesus want to come inside? Let's read Revelation 3:20 together: "Here I am! I stand at the door and knock. If anyone hears my voice and opens the door, I will come in and eat with that person, and they with me."

Did you spot it? Jesus wants to eat with us. The scripture might have said Jesus would come in to heal us, set us free, liberate us, deliver us—and he does all these things—but what Jesus offers us is something even better: intimate fellowship and real food.

People form deep friendships around the dinner table in many cultures, including the ancient Jewish culture. All too often in the US and the UK, we rush our food. We don't chew our food; we gulp it down in ten minutes and rush off to tackle the next item on our never-ending to-do list. This is not the dinner Jesus has in mind. Instead, he invites us to sit, listen, ask questions, tell stories, laugh, cry, or sit silently. We learn to enjoy his presence.

Scripture tells us a great deal about the diets of prophetic people: John the Baptist ate locusts and wild honey (Matt. 3:4); Daniel liked his veggies (Dan. 1:12); ravens fed Elijah with bread and meat (1 Kings 17:6); Isaiah had his mouth touched with burning coal (Isa. 6:6); and Ezekiel ate a scroll tasting as sweet as honey (Ezek. 3:3). However, it is Jeremiah's experience that fascinates me the most. In Jeremiah 15:16, Jeremiah tells the Lord, "When your words came, I ate them; they were my joy and my heart's delight, for I bear your name, Lord God Almighty."

I want Jeremiah's experience. When God speaks, I want to gobble up his words, every crumb, and then lick the plate. I want God's words to bring joy and delight to my heart.

From time to time, I have *imaginary conversations* with Jesus. Sometimes I imagine we are sitting in my living room catching up; sometimes, he walks beside me when I head to the shops; best of all is when I picture Jesus sitting on the other side of a table, ready to share some delicious meal with me. I've been doing this for years. I began this spiritual practice to help me chew on Scripture. Too often, I read Scripture like I eat my food. I rush through a familiar passage, only pausing if some words get stuck in my head like a fish bone in my throat. When I finished reading, I'd put a checkmark beside the passage, and although I had eaten, I certainly was not nourished.

I began to imagine Jesus speaking his words, those red-lettered words printed in our Bibles, directly to me. In my imagination, Jesus didn't rush his words. Frustratingly, he developed the habit of repeating himself, as if I either didn't hear or didn't understand what he was saying the first time. Jesus was like a parent or older sibling cutting up a child's food into small, manageable bites to make them digestible. He taught me to chew.

My imaginary Jesus and I would sit down to eat. He never seemed in a hurry to begin a conversation. He might have started anywhere on my long list of failures, but he didn't. After sitting silently together for some time, he'd often begin by talking about his Father, calling me by name with each point to grab my attention:

> *"Ivan, my Father is the gardener."* (John 15:1)
> *"Ivan, I have loved you even as the Father has loved me. Remain in my love."* (v. 9)
> *"Ivan, my Father is the gardener. He prunes you so you will produce more fruit."* (vv. 1–2)
> *"Ivan, you cannot be fruitful apart from me."* (v. 4)
> *"Ivan, remain in me."* (v. 4)
> *"Ivan, apart from me you can do nothing."* (v. 4)

Every so often, my imaginary Jesus would surprise me, go off script, and emphasize some point or other:

> *"Ivan, apart from me, you can do nothing. Nothing, not one single thing, nothing at all. Zilch."* (v. 4)
> *"Ivan, remain in me."* (v. 4)

We might have sat for a while now. As Jesus spoke to me in my imagination, I'd chase each thought around in my head. "My Father is the gardener." What does a gardener do? I'd remember I'm not much of a gardener. I'm a weeder, trimmer, and grass cutter, but I don't plant or design. I hardly notice the color and scents of the flowers.

> *"Ivan, I am the true vine."* (v. 1)

Remarkably, these imaginary conversations become real. They take on a life of their own. I'd tell Jesus what is going on in my life; where I'm struggling, where I'm hopeful, where I'm thankful and puzzled. I tell him I miss seeing my kids, wish I'd been a better son to my now-departed parents, and how my sports teams are breaking my heart again. I've found that Jesus is a good listener, teaching me how to be one too.

Our conversations are fascinating. On one level, I know I only imagine these moments; Jesus isn't physically sitting across the table from me. Yet, the more I enter these conversations, the more real they become. I've lost count of the number of times the Holy Spirit has livestreamed a word of knowledge, wisdom, a prophetic message, or filled my heart with the gift of faith during our one-sided chat. These imaginary conversations are a form of intimate prayer. I tell Jesus my stuff. Sometimes he tells me what is on his heart. I eat with him, and he eats with me.

The conversational experiences are not unique. A friend recently wrote to me:

> When I read your first book, I could not put it down. I read it through again to digest what you had written, and as I read, I understood because I had come through some of the same experiences. I would read something, think, "That happened

> to me," and then read something else. It was like reading part of my life story you were bringing to remembrance.
>
> Your second book is the same. The way you talk to the Lord is what I do too. I imagine him sitting across from me on the two-seater in my back room, and I chat away. Like you, I imagine his reply, even though I cannot see him physically I see him in my mind's eye, and it is so real. It is when I am listening that He would give me a word of knowledge or a vision of an interpretation of what I had just been praying in the Spirit.

In my imagination, I sometimes ask Jesus what concerns him. To date, he has only told me small but nonetheless important things. Things like, "Ivan, you know Elsie in your church. She's concerned about her sister, Gwen. Ask Elsie how her sister's doing. I'm praying for Gwen. It would mean a lot to Elsie if she knew you were praying for her sister too."

Did you catch that? In my imagination, I heard Jesus say he is praying for Gwen and invited me to join him. It is one thing to know the truth of the scripture that Jesus "always lives to intercede for them" (Heb. 7:25), but this becomes much more real when I realize he is praying for Elsie's sister, Gwen. It had never dawned on me that Jesus might like me to join him in his prayer time. Sometimes I ask him what he is praying about, and sometimes, mysteriously, I get a clue. Jesus is teaching me to pray. You may want to join his prayer meeting too. There's always one happening right where you are. There's one beginning just now.

Activation Exercise 3: Organizing Environments

While we cannot change all our circumstances, that doesn't mean we can do nothing to improve where we are and increase our sensitivity to the Holy Spirit. During one of my attempts to shed a few extra pounds, I read about the importance of organizing the home and work environment to promote healthy eating. The idea was simple: remove unhealthy food from your refrigerator, freezer, cupboards, and countertops so they are not in your line of sight. Then, you'll be less likely to pick them up when your brain goes into auto-snack mode. You know, when you pick up a bag of chips, a cookie, or a candy bar and munch away without consciously thinking about it. By removing the objects of temptation and placing healthier options in our line of sight, we organize our environment to support our decision to eat more nutritious foods.

There's no doubt that our physical environment affects what we think about and how we behave. It's no accident that grocery stores position candy at the checkouts, and department stores position high-value-added perfumes near entrances. Store managers know that most people who buy perfume or candy don't leave home with those products on their shopping lists. People buy them on impulse. Marketing professionals, salespeople, and psychologists all know that the environment matters.

God knows it too. You don't have to dig deeply into Scripture to see how God used symbols, ceremonies, festivals, and songs to direct people's attention toward his covenant. The Sabbath reminded the Israelites to rely on God. The assortment of sacrifices reminded people of their sinfulness and need for cleansing and forgiveness. At various times, the people of God erected stone pillars as a visual reminder of God's covenant. The ark of the covenant, the lavish material in the tabernacle, aromatic incense, ritual washing, musical instruments, and anointing oil all reminded people to turn their attention Godward.

Some twenty years ago, I began *organizing environments* to promote healthy prayer and increase my awareness of the Spirit's work. I started looking for everyday symbols, products, and rituals to remind me of God's goodness. It happened by accident. I was singing "What a Friend We Have in Jesus" in a church service, and I noticed the names of the lyricist Joseph Scriven and the composer Charles

Crozat Converse. *Converse*, I thought, *now there's a familiar name.* In my mind's eye, I could see the athletic shoe manufacturer's logo emblazoned on the side of Converse Chuck Taylor All Star Classic baseball boots. From that moment on, whenever I see the Converse logo on a passerby's footwear, a T-shirt, a TV advert, or a retail store, I remind myself that Jesus is a great friend. I am foolish if I don't bring everything to him in prayer.

I began to look for other everyday objects or actions to incorporate into my prayer life. I was reading Luke's account of the first convert in Europe, Lydia. In Acts 16:13–15, Luke retells the story:

> On the Sabbath we went outside the city gate to the river, where we expected to find a place of prayer. We sat down and began to speak to the women who had gathered there. One of those listening was a woman from the city of Thyatira named Lydia, a dealer in purple cloth. She was a worshiper of God. The Lord opened her heart to respond to Paul's message. When she and the members of her household were baptized, she invited us to her home. "If you consider me a believer in the Lord," she said, "come and stay at my house." And she persuaded us.

There are so many intriguing elements to this passage. The first European convert was female. The Lord opened her heart as she listened to the apostle's teaching, her entire household was baptized, and she showed hospitality to Paul, Silas, and their entourage. As fascinating as these topics are, I was most intrigued by Luke's description of her profession: "a dealer in purple cloth" (v. 14). Luke might have told us that Lydia was a cloth merchant, a women's clothing retailer, or a fancy haberdasher. But he didn't. Luke purposely noted that Lydia was a dealer in purple cloth. *What is so special about purple?* I wondered. Surely orange, red, green, or yellow fabrics are just as good?

One of the challenges of reading Scripture is that we tend to read it with modern eyes. The accessibility of modern English translations can trick us into thinking that the Bible writers are writing to our twenty-first-century culture. Nowadays, we can go into any brick-or-click store and buy clothing of almost any color, including purple. In ancient times, however, purple dye was one of the rarest and most expensive substances, far more valuable than gold. In today's money, experts estimate that one gram of the purple dye used in ancient times would cost $2,700—that's $1,224,693 per pound! In comparison, gold sells at just over $45 per gram or $20,665 per pound. Lydia would have been a rich woman.

In my previous study of Scripture, I'd examined the meaning of various numbers, the importance of towns and cities, the meaning of people's names, or the usage of specific nouns, verbs, or literary embellishments. I had, however, never examined a color, so I began with purple.

I learned that purple dye was rare and expensive because the only known source of purple was from the fluid extracted from tiny Mediterranean Sea snails. Dye manufacturers used 120 pounds of sea snails to produce one gram of dye; that's around four million mollusks to produce one pound.

The first time we see purple mentioned in Scripture is in the context of an offering. In Exodus 25:1–4, God instructs Moses to inform the people what items to include in the offering to weave into the tabernacle curtains and priestly garments: "The LORD said to Moses, 'Tell the Israelites to bring me an offering. You are to receive the offering for me from everyone whose heart prompts them to give. These are the offerings you are to receive from them: gold, silver and bronze; blue, purple and scarlet yarn and fine linen . . .'"

Four verses later, God explains what this offering will accomplish: "Then have them make a sanctuary for me, and I will dwell among them" (v. 8).

God wants to dwell with us. Come, Holy Spirit.

In Esther 8:15, we read that King Xerxes dressed Mordecai in purple after he and Queen Esther thwarted Haman's murderous plot. From Proverbs 31:21–22, we learn that the wife of noble character clothed her family in scarlet but wore purple herself.

Two of the Gospel writers inform us that Roman soldiers dressed Jesus in a purple robe before his crucifixion (Mark 15:17; John 19:2). No wonder the soldiers decided not to quarter the robe; it was simply too valuable to ruin (John 19:24).

So, there we have it, not a scarlet thread, but a purple one. Nowadays, every time I see purple, I remind myself that purple was used in the tabernacle and priestly garments to prepare a place for God to dwell.

Come, Holy Spirit, I pray.

I remind myself that Jesus's death and resurrection made it possible for the Advocate, the Holy Spirit, to come to us (John 16:7).

Come, Holy Spirit.

I remind myself that all those led by the Spirit are sons and daughters of God, making us worthy to wear the purple clothes of rulers.

Come, Holy Spirit.

On another occasion, I noticed that my shampoo contained extra virgin olive oil. *That's interesting,* I thought. *The Bible has much to say about oil; I wonder if I can turn washing my hair into a meaningful prayer time.*

In the Bible, the prophets often symbolized God's calling and anointing by pouring olive oil on the head of the chosen person. As I washed my hair, I began to pray, *Anoint me today to do your work.* This simple practice reminds me that I need God's fresh anointing daily.

Over time, I added other prayers. In Leviticus 24:2, God commanded the Israelites to bring fresh-pressed oil to light the temple lamps and keep them continually burning. *Lord, keep my lamp burning brightly.*

I noticed spiritual leaders often used oil during healing prayer (James 5:14). *Lord, heal me, and let me be used to bring your healing to others.*

In Psalm 23:5, King David sings, "You prepare a table before me in the presence of my enemies; You anoint my head with oil; my cup overflows." *Lord, I need your abundance and victory today.*

Isaiah prophesies the Spirit of the Lord, bringing the oil of gladness instead of mourning (Isa. 61:3). *Lord, fill me with your joy because your joy is strength.*

After Jacob had his dream, he marveled, "Surely the LORD is in this place, and I was not aware of it" (Gen. 28:16).

Jacob anointed his stone pillow with oil (v. 18). *Lord, open my eyes to discern your presence.*

Rinse and repeat!

Questions for Reflection and Discussion

1. In Acts 16:14, we read that the Lord "opened [Lydia's] heart to respond to Paul's message." When has the Lord opened your heart to respond to a message? What was the message? How did you respond?

2. Pick an ordinary experience and work through an Everyday Meditation. Here are the steps to follow:

a) Invite the Holy Spirit to speak to you through the experience.
b) Identify the different stages of your experience. For example, if you choose clothes shopping, you might write a shopping list, drive to the store, try on several outfits, look at your reflection in the mirror, pay at the cash register, and carry your purchases back home.
c) Ask the Lord to bring scriptures to your mind relevant to your experience. Is the Lord speaking to you through these scriptures?

d) Over the next few days, see if the Lord gives you new prophetic insight into your heart or another situation.
e) Write out what you sense God is saying and incorporate your thoughts into your prayer.

3. Pick one of your favorite passages from the Gospels in which Jesus speaks or teaches. Imagine having a conversation with Jesus in which he says these words directly to you. See how the conversation develops. Over the next day or so, see if the Lord gives you new insight into your heart or another situation. How will you respond to his words to you?

4. Can you think of everyday objects you could incorporate in your prayer life in the same way I have included Converse shoes, purple, and olive-oil shampoo in mine?

5. Slowly read John 15:1–17. What words, phrases, or ideas stand out to you? Form a prayer using those themes, inviting God to make them real in your life.

6

Spiritual Forensics

> The word of the Lord came to me: "What do you see, Jeremiah?"
>
> —Jeremiah 1:11a

Ivan, look up.

It was the last day of February 1986. I'd just returned to my apartment following an evening walk around Aston University's campus. I unlocked my door, sat on my bed, and kicked off my shoes. A thought popped into my head.

Ivan, look up.

I was aware of the thought but didn't pay it much attention. I knew what my apartment ceiling looked like:

a rather uninspiring off-white color. I dismissed the idea as another nonsense floating around in my mind. This time, the thought came again, more insistently; I could no longer ignore it. I looked up, expecting to see the same dull bedroom ceiling I'd looked at every morning and evening while lying in my bed. That's not what I saw. Superimposed on the ceiling was a map of Africa, with one area highlighted on the left-hand side of the map, West Africa.

I was unfamiliar with African geography, so I could not identify the country or region highlighted on the map. I studied the map for several seconds before the Lord began a conversation with me in my head. I remembered several accounts of these conversation-like encounters with God in the Old Testament. Abraham dialogued with God when he pleaded for God to spare Sodom (Gen. 18:16–33). Ezekiel's communication with God in the valley of dry bones was conversational (Ezek. 37:1–14). God's commissioning of Jeremiah was a back-and-forth between the prophet and God (Jer. 1:4–19).

The conversation went like this:

Ivan, look up.

I looked up and studied the map.

Ivan, ask me what you see.

That was an odd remark. Ask God what I see. Okay, here goes.

"Lord, what do I see?"

What you see is Sierra Leone. Pray for Sierra Leone.

Ivan, ask me what you see.

Why was the Lord telling me to ask the same question? I wondered. Nonetheless, I asked the question. I've found it's best not to mess with God!

"Lord, what do I see?"

The vision began to change. The picture zoomed in on Sierra Leone like Google Earth zooms in on a region. When the zooming stopped, I saw three movie clip–style visions simultaneously playing on my ceiling, superimposed over the map of Sierra Leone. In one movie clip, I saw human skulls piled up in a massive heap, the empty eye sockets staring at me. In another, I saw rivers of blood seeping into the soil. In the third, I saw a black-like vapor moving across the country. There were images of death everywhere, covering the entire nation.

"What do I see, Lord?" I asked again.

You see a spirit of death moving across Sierra Leone. Pray against this spirit.

Then the Lord said the strangest thing.

Ivan. Ask me to confirm this.

I wasn't sure if "this" referred to the vision of Sierra Leone or a spirit of death. I didn't know.

"Lord, please confirm this."

As suddenly as the vision began, it ended. The map and movie clips disappeared, and I was left staring at my off-white bedroom ceiling again. I immediately picked up a pen and some paper. I began writing down what I had seen and heard in the vision: Sierra Leone, death, skulls, blood, the black cloud, and a spirit of death.

I didn't sleep well that night. I felt an enormous responsibility to pray for Sierra Leone, but I needed to figure out where to start. I knew nothing about the country, its people, challenges, religions, or health issues. I also needed to learn how to pray for anything on this scale. I'd only interceded for individuals and families before. Praying for a nation was an entirely new level of intercessory prayer.

I hadn't been involved in much spiritual warfare and needed to figure out where to begin. Of course, I'd read in Ephesians 6:11–12 that we are engaged in a real spiritual battle: "Put on the full armor of God so that you can take your stand against the devil's schemes. For our struggle is not against flesh and blood, but against the rulers, against the authorities, against the powers of this dark world and against the spiritual forces of evil in the heavenly realms."

I wondered if the "spirit of death" was one of these "spiritual forces of evil in heavenly realms." If it was, how should I pray against it? Scripture identifies different types of evil spirits according to their activity. For example, Paul warned Timothy about deceiving spirits (1 Tim. 4:1). Jesus casts out unclean spirits (Mark 1:25). If a deceiving spirit deceives and an unclean spirit makes a person unclean, I assumed a spirit of death brought death.

The following day my first port of call was the university library. I wanted to find as much relevant information as possible about Sierra Leone. I discovered its capital was Freetown, and I learned a little about its history of slavery. I intended to use this information to help frame my prayers.

After spending an hour or so consulting various encyclopedias and world-fact books, I left the library to visit some friends in one of the high-rise student residences. I walked into the lobby and pressed the elevator button to head to the nineteenth floor. It wasn't long before the elevator dinged, its doors opened, and I walked into the empty elevator. Just as the doors began to close, an African man in his mid-twenties ran in. He pressed one of the floor buttons, and we waited for the doors to close, staring at the numbers above the elevator door. As the doors began to close, this thought went through my head: *This man is from Freetown, Sierra Leone.* The Holy Spirit was livestreaming a word of knowledge. I was standing in an elevator with a man from Sierra Leone's capital city, only a few minutes after learning about Freetown.

I turned to my elevator companion and politely asked, "Excuse me, sir. Are you from Freetown, Sierra Leone?"

He turned to me and gave me the biggest smile. "Yes, I am. Freetown is my home city! Have you been to my country?"

I explained that I had not had the opportunity to travel internationally thus far in my life. If I'd had my wits, I'd have invited him to meet me for tea to learn more about Sierra Leone. I was too slow. He got off on one of the lower-numbered floors, and the elevator doors closed before I thought to invite him.

Aston University's main campus had three thousand residents. It was an international university; students came from all over the world to study. I recognized most students, even if I didn't know all by name. While I had not recognized this man, I assumed I'd meet him again on campus. But I never did, and that puzzled me. Was meeting this Sierra Leonean man the confirmation the Lord had promised? It was certainly unusual.

After visiting some fellow students in their nineteenth-floor apartment, I returned to the ground floor to meet my best friend, Martin, for lunch. We typically walked to a local greasy spoon transport café. The sub sandwiches were enormous, the tea strong, and the prices cheap. I told Martin about the vision and about meeting the guy from

Sierra Leone in the elevator. Martin advised me to pray and see what happened. That's what I did. I included Sierra Leone in my extended times of prayer.

A few days later, I was walking across campus when I saw Martin running to meet me.

"What's up, Martin?" I asked.

"Did you see?" he said breathlessly. "Did you see *The Times* today?" (referencing the London-based newspaper).

"No. Why?

"Yesterday, there was a failed coup d'état in Sierra Leone. Do you think your vision was about that?"

We went to the library together and read articles in the overseas sections of national newspapers. Having read the columns, we both thought it likely that the vision was somehow related to the failed uprising. Martin and I spent time thanking God for his sovereignty and goodness.

I stopped praying for Sierra Leone, as I thought my intercessory work was over. In hindsight, I'm now aware that the Lord never told me to stop praying for Sierra Leone. I assumed I could stop, but I never thought of consulting the Lord on the matter at all.

Intercessory prayer is like holding a kite's tail. When you have the kite's tail firmly in your grasp, you can keep hold of it no matter how the kite tugs or where it twists or turns. However, once you let go, it takes work to catch the kite's tail again. In much the same way, I can maintain an intercessory focus for an extended period, provided I keep a firm grip on the issue in my daily prayers. However, if I prematurely stop praying, the prayer burden often lifts, and I often find it extremely difficult (although not impossible) to regain the spiritual grip essential for effective prayer.

In 1987, there was another failed uprising in Sierra Leone. I didn't know how to pray—the problems seemed overwhelming to me. I couldn't get an intercessory hold on the issue in any meaningful way. Similarly, between 1991 and 2002, Sierra Leone was ravaged by a bloody civil war resulting in seventy thousand casualties and 2.6 million people displaced. Once again, I prayed but never felt I made any spiritual breakthroughs.

I tell this story because it contains insights into how we can grow in our prophetic ministry. I have lived my life exploring what is spiritually possible. Theologically and theoretically, I believe we can shape events through prophetic prayer, but I don't know how to pray this way yet. I keep searching and experimenting using the spiritual forensic approach explained in the following section.

While we may pray daily, we may not grow prophetically every day, week, or month. Nevertheless, no matter when and how the Lord uses us, we must be ready, willing, and able to follow his lead, even into new spiritual territories, as was the case for me through this vision of Sierra Leone. We consistently need to cultivate our ability to use gifts well. My level of giftedness and anointing grows in spurts and then plateaus. The growth-and-plateau cycle continues so long as I keep pressing on. I might see no significant breakthroughs in my prophetic ministry for weeks. Still, advances will surely come if we don't give up.

Spiritual Forensics

Part of my sensitivity to the Holy Spirit stems from my rather unusual conversion experience. I grew up knowing stories about Jesus. I attended children's Sunday school weekly and church services at Easter and Christmas. My parents were not regular churchgoers at this stage in their lives, and when they no longer compelled me to go to church, I stopped attending. By the time I was seventeen years old, I had no Christian friends, attended no religious services, and didn't think about God very much. If my thoughts ever strayed heavenward, I dismissed them. I concluded that Jesus was far less tangible than my record collection, the money in my wallet, and the girls I was interested in dating.

Nothing in my life had prepared me for what happened in late March 1980, a few weeks before my eighteenth birthday.

One afternoon, I was sitting in the guest bedroom of our family home, strumming my guitar. As I was writing some song lyrics, a captivating thought-picture came to mind. I saw myself as a seventeen-year-old kid sitting in the same church pew I had sat in as a five-year-old. I hadn't thought about church for years, so the impression was surprising and unnerving. I shook my head but could not shake the image out. As I looked at the mental picture, two compelling thoughts came to mind. My first thought was to investigate Jesus as an adult and not rely on what I'd learned as a child. As soon as this thought passed through my mind, I instantly became curious about Jesus. I had no way to explain what was happening to me. One second, I had no interest in Jesus, the next, I yearned to know him.

My second thought was even more troubling. In an instant, I wanted to be pure. I'd never given purity much thought. I was a seventeen-year-old boy interested in girls, music, and money. Yet, in the blink of an eye, I knew I was morally filthy and wanted to be pure again. At warp speed, I went from writing a song about goodness-knows-what to desperately wanting to be clean again. I never did get to finish that song. The mental picture disappeared, but the impressions that I needed to investigate Jesus and the desire to be pure both increased exponentially.

It never dawned on me to go to a church to learn about Jesus. Instead, I headed to the local public library. I searched through the library shelves and checked out several books about Jesus. The more I read, the more convinced I became that Jesus was God and had a plan for my life.

I was hooked. I had to follow Jesus. Late at night on April 5, 1980, I took the plunge and told Jesus I wanted to follow him. I woke up the next morning full of joy. Not just happy, but flooded with joy. I was overwhelmed with the love of God. I couldn't stop smiling. The feeling of dirtiness I felt a few days before was gone. I felt clean. God's forgiveness had set me free. I still can't get enough of it!

Becoming a Jesus-follower was exciting but also disturbing. I had no framework to make sense of my encounters with the Spirit. I studied how biblical characters experienced the Holy Spirit's presence differently and began formulating questions to help me analyze my own Holy Spirit encounters. I called this set of questions *spiritual forensics*. I'd seen crime-scene investigators at work in TV detective shows and thought I could learn much about the Holy Spirit by employing the same systematic rigor. There are some significant differences, of course. Forensic investigators examine crime scenes while I examine Holy

Spirit encounters. A crime-scene investigator collects and categorizes blood and bodily fluid stains; hair, threads, and fibers; paint and glass; flammable liquids; firearm evidence, controlled substances; and questionable paper and digital documentation. In contrast, I collected emotions, impressions, locations, bodily sensations, thoughts, and behavior patterns to systematically pay attention to how I and others responded to the Holy Spirit's presence. Whenever I sensed the nearness of the Spirit, I put on the spiritual equivalent of Sherlock Holmes's deerstalker hat, picked up Dr. Watson's bag, and began collecting evidence before other thoughts contaminated the encounter scene.

I began asking myself questions to help me collect evidence of God's presence and see what I might learn from these encounters. Here are some of the questions I developed:

1. Where was I when I sensed the presence of the Holy Spirit? Had I previously perceived the moving of the Holy Spirit in this location or similar places?
2. What was I doing when I became aware of the Holy Spirit's presence?
3. Who was with me? Was I on my own or with other people?

4. If others were present, who were they? Had similar things happened when I was with these same people? Did the other people sense anything, or was it just me? If they felt something, how did they interpret what was going on?
5. How did I know the Holy Spirit was moving? Did I feel anything unusual physically or emotionally? Did I feel peaceful, joyful, shaky, or uptight?
6. What was I thinking about? Did any scriptures or pictures come to my mind? If so, what did I see or hear?
7. What happened to me immediately because of the encounter? Did anything happen later that I can attribute to this encounter?
8. What happened to others? Was anyone healed, set free, or encouraged?
9. How did I sense that the encounter was over? Did I feel heavier or lighter before, during, or after the encounter?
10. Did the encounter change my behavior in any way? Did I want to worship, read the Bible, or run and hide after the encounter?
11. Did the encounter impact others? If so, who and in what way? On what evidence do I draw these

conclusions? Did they say something? Did I observe anything different in their behavior or demeanor?

Let's use my own conversion experience to demonstrate how I use this spiritual forensics approach to examine an encounter with the Holy Spirit.

The first four questions from my spiritual forensics list are easy to answer. I was alone at home, playing guitar, and writing song lyrics. I had no previous visionary experiences.

Question 5: How did I know the Holy Spirit was moving? Did I feel anything unusual physically or emotionally? Did I feel peaceful, joyful, shaky, or uptight?

The picture in my mind's eye was crystal clear, qualitatively different from any thought or idea I'd ever had. Comparing 1970s movie clips on YouTube to today's high-resolution 4K TVs illustrates the qualitative difference in this vision to anything I'd seen before.

Question 6: What was I thinking about? Did any scriptures or pictures come to my mind? If so, what did I see or hear?

I saw a picture of myself as a seventeen-year-old kid sitting in the church pew I sat in as a five-year-old. Along with the picture, I had two compelling thoughts to investigate Jesus as an adult and to be pure.

Question 7: What happened to me immediately because of the encounter? Did anything happen later that I can attribute to this encounter?

As soon as I saw the vision, I wanted to learn about Jesus. It was as if someone had flicked on the get-to-know-Jesus switch in my life. One second, it was off; the next, on. The change in my life was dramatic.

Question 8: What happened to others? Was anyone healed, set free, or encouraged?

I was alone. No one else was immediately impacted.

Question 9: How did I sense that the encounter was over? Did I feel heavier or lighter before, during, or after the encounter?

It's difficult for me to say when the vision ended. On one level, it ended when I stopped seeing the picture of me sitting in the church pew. However, the desire to know Jesus and become pure intensified after the vision ended.

Question 10: Did the encounter change my behavior in any way? Did I want to worship, read the Bible, or run and hide after the encounter?

The encounter led to a massive change in my behavior. I headed to the library the following day and began reading about Jesus. Two weeks later, I became a Jesus-follower. I began to read books about Jesus. I found an old Bible my grandma had given me for my eighth birthday and began to read it. Shortly afterward, I began to attend church.

Question 11: Did the encounter impact others? If so, who and in what way? On what evidence do I draw these conclusions? Did they say something? Did I observe anything different in their behavior or demeanor?

I didn't think anything had happened to anyone else at the time. Twenty years later, however, I reconnected with school friends on social media. I discovered that three old school friends had become Christians due to the authentic changes they had seen in me.

Spiritual forensics has many benefits. First, it helps me to remember the details of my encounters with the Holy Spirit. Second, it allows me to recognize how the Holy Spirit works in and through me. I'm much more vigilant in looking for what I call Holy Spirit clues. Third, it helps me spot new patterns. For example, in the 1990s, I noticed that I experienced a strange tingling sensation at the top of my legs shortly before God healed someone. After seeing the pattern, I consciously paid more attention to what I was feeling in my legs. Whenever I felt this unusual tingling session, I knew God wanted to heal someone. Invariably, I saw people healed. This phenomenon only lasted for six months. I have no idea why it started or stopped, but if it happens again, I'm ready.

Similarly, in the 1990s, I noticed that I could see tiny red laser-point dots on the heads of people to whom I had just prophesied. When I had seen them a few times, I wondered if they were also visible before ministry. Sure enough, they were. Every time I preached over the next six months, I saw these tiny red dots on the foreheads of the people to whom the Lord wanted me to minister that day. One day, for no apparent reason, I no longer saw any dots and haven't seen any since. I have no explanation for why the Holy Spirit used this phenomenon to get my attention. However, had I not employed spiritual forensics, I doubt I would have spotted the pattern.

The earlier we use this forensic approach in our Christian lives, the easier it will be to spot the Holy Spirit's work. Some of us are aware of when we first prophesied. But others begin livestreaming prophetic insight unbeknownst to themselves. My encounter with Ray provides a good example.

Prophesying Unawares

I came second again.

I walked back across the beautiful Trinity College Dublin campus. I said goodbye to the Old Library, the home of the Book of Kells; the Rubrics, where Jonathan Swift lived as a student; and the Samuel Beckett Theater. I walked out through Front Square, hoping someday to return.

My interviews went well. I liked the people. People with very different political views joked together and enjoyed each other's company. What was there not to like about this Top 100 World University? After my final interview, the dean asked me to wait outside while the committee reached its decision. Thirty minutes later, the dean called me back in.

"Thank you for coming, Mr. Filby," he began. "You are a great candidate, and we all enjoyed meeting you. However, we had one exceptional candidate who completed his PhD several years ago. He has more teaching experience and more publications."

My heart sank.

"However," he continued, "we think you have an exciting career in front of you, and we will hope to find grant money to offer you a two-year contract. Here's my card; please keep in touch."

I had hope.

A month earlier, I interviewed at another university. A friend who taught at the university told me about the opening before the dean publicly announced the lectureship. My friend briefed me on what to include in my application packet and told me questions the dean often asked candidates so I could prepare well. After some preliminary conversations, the university chose me as one of their top two candidates and invited me to campus for a final round of interviews. The dean asked the questions I had prepared, and I answered them well. However, the university hired a candidate with much more experience. I was the jobless runner-up. Coming second again at the Trinity College interview rubbed salt in this still-raw wound.

I waved goodbye to Trinity College, grabbed a bite to eat, and walked to a city-center church hosting an evening service.

No sooner had I sat down when a bearded gent wearing a Chelsea Football Club jersey came over to say hello. He told me his name was Ray.

"What brings you to our fair city?" he inquired in his rich Irish brogue.

I told him about my interview at Trinity College, the possibility of a two-year contract, and my excitement to see what God was doing in Ireland.

"No," he said. "This is what is going to happen. The chap offered the position will turn it down, and Trinity College will chase you all over England to make you a job offer."

Yeah, right, I thought. *There's no chance that will happen.*

I flew back home to England. It never dawned on me to send updated contact information to Trinity College Dublin. I lived in Birmingham when I mailed my application. I moved to Nottingham between being called for the interview and traveling to Dublin to meet the business school faculty. I moved again soon after returning from my interview.

Six weeks later, my telephone rang. I was surprised to hear Trinity College's personnel director on the other end of the line calling to offer me the job.

"You're a difficult man to find," she began. "I called your number in Birmingham. The tenants there gave me your new phone number in Nottingham. I called that number, only to find you had moved again. I'm glad I finally reached you. After accepting the position, the other candidate had second thoughts and turned down our job offer. I want to offer you the Lecturer in Business Studies position. Welcome to Trinity College."

So, the prophetic word given in the Dublin church was accurate. The first-choice candidate did turn down Trinity's job offer. Trinity College had to "chase" me around England, calling three telephone numbers before finally tracking me down.

Several months after moving to Dublin, I decided I should thank the bearded Chelsea fan who assured me the job would be mine. After phoning a few friends, I discovered Ray's phone number and called him one evening.

"Hi, Ray. My name is Ivan Filby. I don't know if you'll remember me. After interviewing at Trinity College, I met you at a Friday night meeting in the Academy Theater."

"Oh, hi, Ivan! I do remember. What's up?"

"I just wanted to thank you for the prophetic word you gave me that night."

"Who me? I've never prophesied in my life."

"You know, the prophesy about the first-choice candidate turning down Trinity's job offer and Trinity chasing me all over England."

"Did I say that? I honestly don't remember. Likely, I said it to encourage you. You looked kind of disappointed."

I interrupted Ray and told him I was lecturing at Trinity College and that the university had to call three telephone numbers to track me down eventually. I thanked him again, and we ended the call after some good Irish slagging (ridiculing) of each other's favorite soccer teams.

Over the years, I've given Ray's prophecy much thought. It strikes me as odd that Ray, who began our conversation so emphatically with, *this is what is going to happen,* was utterly oblivious to the fact that he had prophesied. Perhaps he had prophesied before and was equally unaware. Had he used a forensic approach, he would have been more aware of how the Lord was using him, allowing him to nurture his gifting better.

Spiritual Forensics Addendum

I pray with Paul Sunderland, professor of worship arts at Greenville University, in our weekly Zoom meeting. We attended a New Room Conference together, heard about the importance of prayer bands, and started our own. He encouraged me as I wrote this book, and I told him the questions I use in my spiritual forensics audit. He suggested I add one more: After an encounter with the Holy Spirit, do you struggle with any temptations or sins?

What an insightful question. We know from Scripture that Elijah ran away directly after his encounter with the prophets of Baal (1 Kings 19:3), the devil tempted Jesus in the wilderness after his baptism in the Jordan River (Matt. 4:1–11), and James and John struggled with pride (Mark 10:37). Asking this question and having a prayer partner to nudge us when we get spiritually sleepy are great ways to help us guard our hearts.

Questions for Reflection and Discussion

1. Use the spiritual forensics questions to analyze some of your encounters with the Lord. What did you learn from asking these questions?

2. How did you become a follower of Jesus? Write out or tell your story.

3. Have you ever given or heard a prophecy? How did you weigh the prophecy? What parts of the prophecy helped you the most?

4. After an encounter with the Holy Spirit, do you struggle with any temptations or sins? Bring them to the Lord.

5. Ray prophesied without knowing what he was saying. What does this story teach us about God and prophetic ministry?

7

Prophetic Ministry and God's Good Plans

"For I know the plans I have for you," declares the LORD, "plans to prosper you and not to harm you, plans to give you hope and a future."
—Jeremiah 29:11

Not again! I couldn't believe it.

I was standing at Heathrow Airport's Terminal One baggage claim waiting for our cases to arrive. Kathie had slipped off to find coffee, and I watched the empty belt slow down and stop before my eyes. Happy passengers had already collected their luggage. I was left alone, bagless, and wondering how I would break the bad news to Kathie.

This is not how I imagined our tenth wedding anniversary would begin.

It wasn't the first time an airline had mishandled our baggage. Our luggage didn't arrive on time for our honeymoon either. We landed in Cape Town, only to discover our luggage was on its way to Paris. The airline took five days to deliver our bags to our hotel room.

Our tenth wedding-anniversary trip was a surprise. Each year, either Kathie or I organize our wedding anniversary on an alternate-year basis. I planned our first wedding-anniversary trip to London; Kathie planned the following year's getaway, and so on. Ten was an even number, so it was Kathie's turn. Our children were only eight and six then, so I anticipated we would be heading to a hotel somewhere in Ireland. That's what we did most years.

On our anniversary morning, I dumped my overnight bag into our car's back seat, and we headed off. I was curious if we'd be heading south from our Dublin home into County Wicklow, west toward Connemara, or north to Skerries or Malahide. We loved these places, offering beautiful coastal views and inland tapestries of green fields and hedgerows.

Kathie headed north. *Great*, I thought, *Malahide or Skerries.*

It turned out to be neither. Instead of going straight over the roundabout at Dublin Airport to Malahide, she turned left into the airport and parked. She opened the car's trunk and pulled out two suitcases she'd sneakily packed the day before. She popped my overnight bag into the car's trunk and shut the lid. "You won't be needing that," she teased.

Kathie checked us in at the Aer Lingus counter and handed me my boarding pass for London. This was a surprise, but it was a rather nice one. London is one of my favorite cities, where we celebrated our first wedding anniversary. One night in London would be a treat, as much as we could afford on our tight budget.

Kathie rejoined me at the luggage belt. I gave her the bad news about our luggage. Instead of being upset, she laughed, and said, "Our bags were not tagged for Heathrow. We're only transferring flights here. I only asked you to wait for the luggage for fun. You should have seen your face when our cases didn't arrive! Let's get some lunch."

Over lunch, I peppered Kathie about our destination, but she batted all my questions away. I knew we had to pay some large bills at the end of the month, and I was concerned about how much this anniversary trip would cost. I didn't want to mention my financial concerns to

Kathie, as I knew she must have spent considerable time planning our trip.

Kathie handed me my next boarding pass, to Nice, on the French Riviera. I began to do back-of-the-envelope mental arithmetic, trying to figure out how we could pay for this romantic getaway. No matter how I did the calculations, I knew we would need a small loan to pay our end-of-the-month bills.

And the costs began to escalate!

When we arrived at the car rental desk, Kathie introduced herself to the agent and mentioned that she had reserved a rental car for five days. Five days! What was she thinking? I had crucial work meetings scheduled back in Dublin in three days. We couldn't stay for five days. I hadn't booked vacation time at work, and we couldn't afford five days on the French Riviera even if I had.

Kathie smiled and said, "I've worked everything out with your assistant. Your calendar is clear until Wednesday. Relax. We are on our second honeymoon."

We pulled our luggage to the rental car, and Kathie drove us to Cannes, the home of the Cannes Film Festival. She pulled up outside a beautiful boutique hotel, and we checked in. Cha-ching!

After unpacking, Kathie said, "I have some explaining to do. Let's get something to eat." We walked down old, cobbled streets and found a sunny table outside a quaint restaurant. After the waiter had taken our order, Kathie began, "Happy anniversary! I love you and understand you well enough to know you are panicking about how we'll pay for this trip, aren't you?"

I nodded. Kathie smiled and continued, "No need to worry; I've paid for everything. All you need to do is enjoy it. It's my gift to you."

I smiled weakly.

I knew Kathie could not have paid for this anniversary trip. She only worked a couple of hours each day to help with our expenses—she'd decided to stay home for the kids while they were still young. If Kathie had paid for this trip, she'd either secured a loan from her parents or the bank, and in both cases, we'd have to pay it back, but at least not at the month's end.

Kathie took a sip of sparkling water, dipped some bread into olive oil, and began to tell her story.

"I've been planning this for over ten years. Just before our wedding, I decided I wanted to take you away for our tenth anniversary and pay for everything so you wouldn't have to worry about finances. Right after we married, I set up a secret bank account you knew nothing about and saved a little from our housekeeping budget every month. I've saved for ten years. I've covered the flights, our hotel, and the rental car.

I have enough cash for our meals, and we will have enough money left for a few little excursions. Happy anniversary!"

I was dumbstruck. I've never felt so loved. Kathie had planned and sneakily saved for ten years to make this second honeymoon possible.

"It was tough to save at times," she confessed. "When the mortgage interest rate went up, I was tempted to tell you about this pot of money. But I didn't. I knew we'd find another way to cover the increased mortgage payments, and we did. When we needed extra money to cover the unanticipated costs of our house repairs, I thought I might have to use my secret stash. But I didn't. I knew I could only spend the money once and I wanted to use it for our tenth wedding anniversary. So, I kept secretly saving, and you knew nothing about it, Mr. Professor of Business!"

We had a fantastic anniversary. We took a memorable boat trip to St. Tropez and had dinner one night under orchestrated fireworks. We walked along the sandy beaches, hand in hand. What made it most remarkable, though, was that Kathie had planned everything, including how to cover the cost. She couldn't believe I had not figured out what she was doing right under my nose. It was a complete surprise and five of the best days of my life.

I hear you say, "What a quaint story, but what has it to do with me?" Nothing and everything! It's our love story, so on one level, it has nothing to do with you whatsoever. Hands off; keep out! But on another level, it has everything to do with you. Let me explain it this way: Have you ever heard a young father tell a group of friends how he understands more about God's fatherly heart after the birth of his baby? I'm sure new mothers say the same things too. If you are a parent, I'm sure you can remember your overwhelming love for your newborn. Your child was so helpless, so dependent. I bet you did not know your heart could be so full of love. When we find that quality of love in our hearts, we get a fresh glimpse of how God loves us, don't we?

Now, with that thought in mind, let's return to the French Riviera. One afternoon, while Kathie was journaling, I walked alongside Cannes harbor. I was certainly overwhelmed by Kathie's love for me and her ten years of secret planning. But what captured my attention even more was thinking about God's plans for me. God has not been secretly planning for only ten years, as remarkable as that is. He's been planning since before time began.

God's Good Plans

It's difficult to imagine how God does his planning. I'm guessing God doesn't use some divine spreadsheet in which he places every person in an individual cell. It is far more intimate than that. The marvelous but difficult--to-grasp good news is that God knows each of us intimately. He knows what is ultimately good for each of us, and when we accept God's good for us, his goodness, everyone benefits.

The apostle Paul gives us a glimpse of God's planning in his letter to the fledgling church in Ephesus. Paul writes that God "chose us in [Jesus] before the creation of the world to be holy and blameless in his sight" (Eph. 1:4). Isn't that beautiful? I think so. He chose us in Jesus Christ before he had flung Mars into space or created the beauty we see in photographic images from the James Webb Space Telescope.

It's clear from Scripture that God intends some of his plans to be for us all. Others are bespoke, just for us individually. In a real sense, God doesn't want some of us to enjoy lives of holiness and others to limp along, crippled by ongoing sin. No, not at all. How God works out this plan in our lives might differ, but he puts a checkmark against each of our names in his "intended for holiness" list. To the extent that you allow God to work out this plan in your life is the extent to which you surrender to him.

In the West, our self-centeredness tricks us into believing God's primary concern is our happiness. It is not.

God did not choose us in Christ before the foundation of the world to be happy, but rather holy and blameless. Joy comes from surrender.

If we want to know God's good plans, Romans 12:1–2 has much to teach us:

> Therefore, I urge you, brothers and sisters, in view of God's mercy, to offer your bodies as a living sacrifice, holy and pleasing to God—this is your true and proper worship. Do not conform to the pattern of this world, but be transformed by the renewing of your mind. Then you will be able to test and approve what God's will is—his good, pleasing and perfect will.

We will know God's will—his plans—only when we offer our lives fully to him, resist worldly pressures to mold us in any shape but Christ's, and allow his love to wash our minds. And when we discover God's plans for us this way, we find them to be *good, pleasing, and perfect.*

We do not get a say in some of God's plans for us. We don't get to choose our biological parents; we can't select the color of our skin or eyes. While debating with philosophers in Athens, Paul clarified that God marked out everyone's time in history and geographical location (Acts 17:26). Still, we don't know how he reached these decisions. We can't figure out why we were born in the twentieth or twenty-first century and not in the first, tenth, or seventeenth. What we can be sure of, however, is that whenever or wherever we were born, God intends that in that time and place, we "seek him and perhaps reach out for him and find him, though he is not far from any one of us" (v. 27). In God's wisdom, he desires us all to be like Esther, born for "such a time as this" (Est. 4:14).

Joseph knew this to be true. He didn't choose to be sold into slavery by his brothers. Joseph didn't opt in to be falsely accused of sexual impropriety, imprisoned, or promoted to run Egypt's famine management plan. He didn't even choose his prophetic gifting. But Joseph did make choices. He chose to use his gifting for good. He decided not to take revenge on Potiphar's wife. He refrained from punching Pharoah's chief cupbearer on the nose for forgetting about him and leaving him in jail for two more years. He forgave his brothers, who dropped him down a pit and sold him into slavery.

Joseph's prophetic gifting helped him see the bigger picture. When his brothers come to meet Joseph, hoping to buy grain, Joseph tells them, "And now, do not be distressed and do not be angry with yourselves for selling me here, because it was to save lives that God sent me ahead of you" (Gen. 45:5). Later, he says, "You intended to harm me, but God intended it for good to accomplish what is now being done, the saving of many lives" (50:20).

Joseph demonstrates for us a prophetic ministry seasoned with grace. But he also shows us much more. He acknowledges God sent him ahead of his brothers. But he got no first-class ticket to Egypt. He recognizes his brothers' intentions to harm him and sell him into slavery were all part of God's plan. Joseph recognizes that God's good plans are not always the ones we might choose for ourselves.

It's likely Joseph learned something else too. When Joseph was a young man, still living at home, God gave him two dreams about his father and brothers all bowing down to him (Gen. 37). We don't know whether he thought about this dream in Egypt. We know he remembered it when his brothers knelt before him, asking for grain (42:9). Joseph could never have imagined God would fulfill this prophetic dream this way. We have much to learn from this. If God speaks to us, we need to hold on to his word tightly, but hold any ideas about how God might fulfill these promises very loosely. When God speaks, our minds often race to figure out how God will carry out his plans for us. We must never forget that God is full of surprises and his ways are higher than ours (Isa. 55:8–9).

Journey Interrupters

God often speaks only in whispers, easily missed if we are not paying attention. These livestreams include prophecy, but God might just as easily use Scripture, a song, or the words of a friend to speak to us gently. If we keep missing these whispers, God sometimes uses *journey interrupters* to get our attention. Journey interrupters work like spiritual railway switches (railway points, to Brits like me). Here's the idea. We are racing down the track heading in one direction when God has an entirely different destination for us in mind. We might be trundling along on autopilot, falling asleep at the wheel, and missing God's change-direction signs. The need to change direction is urgent. Perhaps danger lies ahead. Maybe he has passengers for us to collect along the way. Possibly God has a new assignment, and we need to adjust our destination mid-course. What will God do? In my case, he has sometimes used visions and voices to interrupt my journey before I miss the opportunity to alter course.

We can find many biblical examples of journey interrupters. Joseph was about to divorce Mary quietly; God interrupted him with a dream in which an angel told him Mary's child was conceived by the Holy Spirit (Matt. 1:19–21). Elisha's servant was about to flee when he saw the strength of the Aramean army; God interrupted him with a vision showing him the greater power of God's angelic army (2 Kings 6:15–17). Moses was happily tending his father-in-law's flock when God interrupted him with a vision of a burning bush, calling him to go back to Egypt to lead the Israelites to freedom (Ex. 3).

God interrupt us, not just because he loves us, but because he wants to bless others. If we don't change direction, others will lose out. If we miss God's whispers and journey interrupters, we miss out too. God doesn't always call us to easy things, but we are always blessed when we change direction to join God in his work.

Billy Jenkins

I was dating Anna, my cute seventeen-year-old girlfriend, when I became a Jesus-follower in 1980. She didn't share my excitement for Jesus, so we quickly parted ways. However, while I didn't see Anna much for the next couple of years, I didn't stop thinking about her. I imagined my feelings for her would dissipate, but they didn't. I wondered what she was doing, who she might be dating, and whether she was happy. I began to pray for her. Throughout my four years at university, I didn't date. I studied, and I prayed for Anna.

During the first year of my doctoral studies, I received an invitation to Anna's twenty-first birthday party in the mail. I'd only had limited contact with Anna for several years, so the letter was a surprise. However, her celebration coincided with a university holiday. I had already planned to go back home to meet my parents, and I agreed to pop into her birthday party for a few minutes to say hello.

When I rang the doorbell, Anna answered and introduced me to her fiancé. Another surprise. I stayed for about an hour, chatted with Anna and her fiancé, and caught up with some mutual friends. Anna seemed happy. Her fiancé was a good match for her. Finally, I could move on.

I stopped praying for Anna.

A couple of months later, Anna sent me a letter.

"I've become a Christian," she wrote. "When you came to my birthday party, there was something very different about you. You were so joyful and peaceful. I began to wonder if there was a God."

By the time I'd read these opening lines of her letter, I was leaping around the room. I calmed down and read some more.

"Anyway, I recently gave my life to Jesus. It was extraordinary. I felt like a big hand was moving inside me, scraping out all the junk in my life. I feel so free. I love Jesus."

I was ecstatic. We spoke a couple of times on the telephone. It wasn't long before she ended her engagement, and we soon began dating again. In my mind, it was clear we were meant for each other. I could see the storyline: a man comes to Christ and prays for his ex-girlfriend for five years. She becomes a Christian. They date again, get married, and live happily ever after.

I helped Anna find a church. She had never attended a church service, so I went with her, and introduced her to Dave, the pastor, and Billy Jenkins, the worship leader.

A week or so later, I set aside some days to pray and fast. The question I wanted the Lord to answer was simple: Should I ask Anna to marry me while I was still studying for my doctorate, or should I wait until I'd graduated and was financially more secure?

I'd never fasted before and was still trying to figure out what to do other than pray and not eat. I set aside three days to fast and pray. On the first day, I walked around my neighborhood. I prayed and prayed some more. I repeatedly asked the Lord, "When should I ask Anna to marry me?"

I spent the second day in my room. All my housemates were away, so I had the house to myself. I went down to the living room to pray at five in the evening. The house was so still and peaceful. I could sense the beautiful presence of the Holy Spirit in the room as I prayed. I knelt in the middle of the floor, lifted my hands in worship, and waited quietly in case the Lord wanted to speak.

A few minutes later, I heard what seemed to be an audible voice. I was so surprised that I jumped; I knew no one else was in the house. I knew it was the Lord livestreaming, and I didn't much care for what he had to say. All I heard was a name: *Billy Jenkins.*

Along with the name came the strongest impression: *Billy Jenkins will be Anna's husband.*

I shook my head and convinced myself that my imagination was playing tricks on me. This couldn't be God's voice, I reasoned. I had prayed for Anna for five years and only introduced her to Billy a few days before. I prayed once more. Again, I heard the voice, and again, I jumped.

Ivan, Billy Jenkins will be Anna's husband.

Two weeks later, Anna ended our relationship.

Ten months later, Anna married Billy Jenkins.

In hindsight, after more than thirty beautiful years married to Kathie, I'm grateful the Lord interrupted my plans. But at that time, I was devastated. I couldn't sleep. I wished I'd never begun my fast. I complained to God, explaining he was unfair. I was left hurt and confused. I wondered how I could have been so stupid. I should have taken her to a different church. I should have never introduced her to Billy. Why had God allowed this? Could I ever trust my own heart again? Could I even trust God?

God's plans are always good for us, even if they sometimes appear differently.

Pastor Jerry

In chapter 1, we saw how wonderful it is when God tells us he has heard the cry of our hearts. Sometimes, however, we cannot articulate our own heart's cries. Something may not be quite right, but we cannot put our finger on what it is. We may feel left entirely in the dark by current circumstances, without knowing why we are experiencing our various trials or what they might accomplish. Most of us have experienced such times. In these times, a word from the Lord can help us make sense of our experiences and get a glimpse into the Lord's perspective on our current life situation.

I felt left in the dark for most of 2021. I resigned as president of Greenville University in May 2020, at the beginning of the Covid pandemic, partly because of a prophetic word we received indicating that God had a new assignment for us. Our time at the university in Illinois needed to end. Like Abraham, we had yet to learn where we would be heading or what we would be doing. Several times I prayed John Wesley's Covenant Prayer:

I am no longer my own, but thine.
Put me to what thou wilt,
rank me with whom thou wilt.
Put me to doing, put me to suffering.
Let me be employed by thee or laid aside by thee,
exalted for thee or brought low for thee.
Let me be full, let me be empty.
Let me have all things, let me have nothing.
I freely and heartily yield all things
to thy pleasure and disposal.
And now, O glorious and blessed God,
Father, Son, and Holy Spirit,
thou art mine, and I am thine.
So be it.
And the covenant which I have made on earth,
let it be ratified in heaven.
Amen.

I remember praying, somewhat rhetorically, *Let me be used by thee or set aside by thee*, wondering where God might deploy me next. However, in many ways, 2021 was a year of being set aside. I had plenty to do. I remained engaged in US higher education for a couple of days each week. I completed the manuscript of my first book, *Livestream: Learning to Minister in the Power of the Holy Spirit*. I was appointed as a licensed pastor to assist Kathie in leading Towerview Church in Bangor, Northern Ireland. I was busy, but I felt emotionally raw and set aside.

There's much to learn in these fallow seasons. Our pride gets a therapeutic hammering when we realize we may need to remain on the bench. That doesn't make the experience any more manageable, particularly when we do not understand why and can't fathom what God is doing, which is often the case.

Occasionally, God shines light into our darkened understanding. In September 2021, I was worshipping in the congregation at Towerview Church, just a few weeks before I was due to fly to the US to attend the New Room Conference. In the middle of worship, a thought suddenly popped into my mind: *Would Pastor Jerry have a prophetic word for me at New Room?*

It was a reasonable thought. At two previous New Room conferences, God had used Pastor Jerry very powerfully to livestream God's love to me during some very challenging times in my presidency at Greenville University. In 2018, Jerry sought me out three times to pray for me and encourage me with Psalm 30:5: "For his anger lasts only a moment, but his favor lasts a lifetime; weeping may stay for the night, but rejoicing comes in the morning."

Each time Jerry prayed, God's love overwhelmed me. Jerry's livestreams gave me hope in a time of brokenness. My challenges did not lessen, but I found new strength to tackle them.

The following year I was emotionally healthier and thought nothing of allowing Jerry to pray for me again. We bumped into each other just before one evening service at New Room. He showed me pictures of a new grandbaby. I thanked him for his ministry the previous year. Before we headed to our seats, Jerry placed his hand on my shoulder and said, "Let me pray for you, Ivan." Instantly, I had a vision of God's love for Greenville University. Once again, I was overwhelmed by the love of God, this time for the university I was leading. I wept continually for the next twenty-four hours. That wasn't too much of a problem at the Christian conference. It was far more embarrassing on the drive home. It's hard to order a double tall extra dry cappuccino and a tall flat white at Starbucks with tears streaming down your cheeks.

So there I was, two years later, standing in a church service, with my hands in the air, worshipping, wondering if the Holy Spirit would use Jerry to bring perspective on my feelings of being set aside. I tried to push this thought into the back of my mind, planning to process it after the church service ended, but the impression only strengthened.

Then the oddest thing happened. I had a vision of Jerry standing next to me in the service, prophesying over me. I had my eyes closed and knew it was a vision, but it was very realistic; I could even feel Jerry's hand resting on my shoulder. Then, in my vision, Jerry livestreamed a most helpful word of wisdom to me: "Ivan," said Jerry, "this is what the Lord says: 'Ivan, you know when you need to repaint an external door or window frame?'" I knew all too well. Painting is not a task I particularly enjoy. Truth be told, I tend to cut corners. "You do the bare minimum to prepare the wood. You quickly sand it, clean it with a damp cloth, and slap on a new coat of paint. You're always in a rush." That was true. I never took the time to remove the previous paint, sand down the surface, apply an undercoat, and then a final gloss or varnish. I want things done quickly to move on to my next chore. "Ivan, I'm not like that at all. I want to apply a new coat on you. It will be completely, remarkably different. I remove all the coats of paint that cover you. Oh, and by the way, I'm a master craftsman. I never rush. I do things properly and carefully. I want the new paint, this new anointing, to stick and not peel off in the heat of the day."

So, in the generosity of his heart, God livestreamed a word of wisdom to me in a vision. I was not expecting a vision like this; it had never happened before, nor since.

I do not know why God chose to communicate with me this way. He could have spoken quietly to my heart during a time of prayer. Perhaps he had already tried, and I wasn't listening. I am, however, grateful for the word of wisdom that helped me make sense, at least in part, of what God was doing during this period of feeling set aside.

I'm grateful for the insight, but I'm not too fond of it. I keep offering to lend God a whole line of power tools to speed up the sanctification process. So far, God has ignored my offers of help. He's an old-school master craftsman intent on doing things his way, doing them well and right. I must learn to wait on the Lord. God won't let us cut corners when he is in charge.

I met Pastor Jerry again at the 2021 New Room Conference. Without going into much detail, I did tell him of my vision. He smiled, lifted his hands in worship, and said, "Praise the Lord!"

People sometimes ask whether these direction-changing experiences are a sign of deep spirituality. My answer is no. They may indicate the exact opposite. Likely, God had tried several other ways to reach me, but I didn't see or hear them. We must be cautious in assuming that people with unique spiritual experiences are somehow more holy or blessed. There's no evidence for this from Scripture. Remember what Jesus said to Thomas when he finally met the risen Savior: "Because you have seen me, you have believed; blessed are those who have not seen and yet have believed" (John 20:29).

I can't imagine a more profound spiritual experience than meeting the risen Christ physically after his resurrection and before his ascension to heaven. Yet, Jesus says those who didn't have this experience, yet believed, were very blessed indeed. The mark of maturity is not whether you have such experiences, but whether you walk in faith and obedience, allowing the Holy Spirit to make you more Christlike.

Questions for Reflection and Discussion

1. Has God ever put a journey interrupter in your way? If so, what happened?

2. Slowly pray John Wesley's Covenant Prayer. Which parts are the hardest for you to pray? Why do you think this is?

3. Think back over your life. Can you think of times God clearly led you? What happened? How did you respond?

4. In what ways have you been born for "such a time as this" (Est. 4:14)? Are there people in your circle of influence to

whom God may want to use you to reveal his heart? Ask the Lord to give you a verse of Scripture, a prophetic insight, or a word of encouragement for them. Think about the best way to communicate this to them, and record what happened when you passed on the insight.

5. Ephesians 1:4 tells us that before he created anything, God "chose us in him before the creation of the world to be holy and blameless in his sight." Why do you think holiness is such a big deal for God?

8

Ministering Freedom

> Above all else, guard your heart,
> for everything you do flows from it.
> —Proverbs 4:23

I don't know what to do. David used to love school. He's always been a happy child. But this has been going on for several weeks now. We are at our wit's end. We don't know how to help him."

I sat in Helen's suburban kitchen, talking about David, her seven-year-old son. Helen had been happily married for many years, and David was their youngest of three boys. Helen told me that David had always been a happy child who loved kindergarten and adapted quickly to "big" school. He was outgoing and popular. Yet, a few weeks earlier, his behavior changed. Helen was holding David's hand, walking him toward the school, when David unexpectedly grabbed the school gates and gripped the black iron railings so tightly that his little knuckles turned white. David began to scream and weep in a symphony of unhappiness. Helen later confided that she was both embarrassed and concerned. Had David been bullied at school? Had his teacher reprimanded him? What was going on?

Eventually, Helen pried David's fingers from the school gate, and they walked to class. Helen had a quick word with his teacher, who seemed equally puzzled by David's behavior. David's teacher confirmed that he was neither in trouble nor had been bullied. She said, "David is well-adjusted, popular, and eager to learn. Look! He's happily playing with his friends. Perhaps he just got out of the wrong side of his bed this morning."

Sure enough, David was soon playing some make-believe games with his friends.

Helen left the classroom far happier. After the three boys were safely tucked up in bed that evening, she mentioned the incident to her husband, Bryan. She thought about it no more until the following day when David grabbed the school gates again and began screaming. After calming him down, gently opening his fingers, and walking him into the classroom, Helen spoke with David's teacher. Was she sure nothing had happened to David at school that might explain this behavior? Had he fallen out with any of his friends?

Once again, his teacher pointed to David and commented that David always seemed happy in class. "He always does what I ask him to do. He can be a little loud sometimes, but he seems well-adjusted," she said. His teacher showed Helen some of David's drawings on the classroom wall and assured her that David seemed fine. "I'm sure he'll be fine tomorrow morning."

David seemed normal when Helen met him at the school gates after school, and he chatted enthusiastically about some papier-mâché modeling he had been doing in class. Helen was thankful that David seemed happy—and that she didn't have to clear up the messy classroom after twenty or so seven-year-olds had worked on their paper, water, and flour artistic creations!

But David's distressing behavior didn't cease. Every morning he'd grab the school gate and scream at the top of his voice. Helen told me he'd cry and sob as if his life depended upon it. Helen spoke with the school principal. She assured Helen that David was fine when he was at school. Helen made an appointment with their family doctor. After a thorough examination, the family practitioner confirmed that David seemed fine. Despite these assurances, David's distressing behavior did not stop.

Helen sighed. "Ivan, will you pray for David? You seem to have a knack for this type of thing."

I had no such knack. I'd seen a few people physically healed, but this deep inner healing was new territory for me. I was twenty-five at the time, unmarried, with no kids. Ministering to children was well beyond my experience or comfort zone. I had no idea what was distressing David; I had no idea how to pray and felt out of my depth. I've since discovered that feeling out of our depth is where God likes us to be. We see most breakthroughs when we are most dependent on him and less influenced by our past formulas, successes, and failures.

I asked the Holy Spirit to help me understand what was causing David's distress. I wanted to know what was going on in David's soul, spirit, or body to figure out how to pray for him. I kept asking for a word of knowledge, but one never came. Up until this time, I relied on words of knowledge to know how to begin ministry times. If the Lord revealed what troubled people, I'd be in a better position to know how to pray. However, the only thought that bubbled up was a movie clip of David fast asleep in his bed, with his dad, Bryan, and me kneeling beside his bedside, asking the Holy Spirit to flood David with peace. I found the picture encouraging but not helpful. It contained no information on what troubled David, so I kept praying for more insight. None came.

After receiving no additional insight, I shared with Helen and Bryan the only sense I had received, and they agreed to let me pray for David when he was asleep. Around nine o'clock that evening, I walked to their house. Bryan and I tiptoed upstairs and knelt beside David's bed. I whispered my prayers: "Lovely Holy Spirit, bring your deep peace into all the hidden areas of David's life. We welcome you. Holy Spirit, bring your peace, the peace of heaven, into David's life. Chase away all darkness. Flood him with your holy light."

As we were tiptoeing back downstairs, I had the strongest impression that we'd need to repeat these prayers several days in a row. I asked permission to call the following evening, the next, and the next still. It was as if these prayers were like chemotherapy to David's soul; he needed to complete the entire course of prayer treatment for the healing to take hold. We prayed four or five times over ten days. A few days after our final time of prayer, Helen called. She was so excited and gushed, "This morning, David didn't grab the school gate, scream, or sob. He just ran up to the school door, waved quickly, and joked with some friends inside the school hallway. David's distressing behavior has stopped."

Here's what's interesting: Helen, Bryan, and I never knew what disturbed David. We didn't know if he had experienced some trauma, was attacked by some evil spirit, or was struggling with inner concerns he could not express. Nonetheless, even though I never knew the cause of David's behavior, it didn't matter. God still touched him where he needed to be touched. Every time Bryan and I prayed, a deep peace became tangibly present in David's bedroom.

Here's what happened. Instead of livestreaming a word of knowledge to help me understand what was triggering David's behavior, the Holy Spirit gave me a *word of wisdom* to show me how to pray. God can livestream whatever gifts he chooses to accomplish what is on his heart. We must hear his voice and follow along, keeping in step with the Spirit.

In 1 Corinthians 2:10b–13, we read these beautiful words:

> The Spirit searches all things, even the deep things of God. For who knows a person's thoughts except their own spirit within them? In the same way no one knows the thoughts of God except the

> Spirit of God. What we have received is not the spirit of the world, but the Spirit who is from God, so that we may understand what God has freely given us. This is what we speak, not in words taught us by human wisdom but in words taught by the Spirit, explaining spiritual realities with Spirit-taught words.

In some mysterious way, the Holy Spirit searches the *deep things of God* and *the thoughts of God*. He then communicates tiny fragments of God's love, wisdom, and understanding. In David's case, the Spirit revealed that God wanted to minister a new quality of peace to David. As Bryan and I followed the Spirit's lead, we got to share this peace too.

Ministry Paths

I hadn't thought about Helen, Bryan, or David for thirty years until I sat with another tired young couple. Maggie and Ben had toilet-trained their three-year-old son, Owen. However, after several months of dry nights, he began to wet his bed again.

Maggie explained, "I'm exhausted, Ivan. Every night I'm up at least once, stripping Owen's bedding, changing his pajamas, settling him down again, and then trying to get back to sleep. Every morning I have an extra load of laundry to wash and dry, ready for nighttime emergencies."

Maggie continued: "Owen slept through the night dry for months until Ben's accident. I'm sure that's what is upsetting him."

Two months earlier, Ben, a keen motorcycle enthusiast, had a near-fatal motorbike accident when an automobile driver sideswiped him at a busy intersection. After several surgeries, he came home in a wheelchair with his ankles and legs joined with plates, rods, and screws. Since his father's accident, Owen had wet the bed most nights, sometimes two or three times. Maggie was exhausted.

During our conversation, I prayed with Maggie and Ben. I placed my hand on Ben's ankles and prayed for healing. While praying for Ben, I thought of Helen, Bryan, and David for the first time in years. I prayed for them so long ago that remembering their names took me some time. *Why was I thinking about them while praying with Maggie and Ben?* I wondered. I could only conclude that the Holy Spirit was inviting me to pray for Owen in the same way I had prayed for David.

I told Maggie and Ben about my prayer times with David, and asked if they would be willing for me to pray for Owen every time I called around to their house. They agreed.

Ben hobbled upstairs, and I followed him into Owen's room. He was sound asleep. I whispered my prayer: "Precious Holy Spirit, come and rest upon Owen. Bring your peace into his innermost parts. Drive out every fear. Precious Holy Spirit, help Owen experience your peace. Let your peace penetrate his mind and emotions. Let your peace reach the hidden parts of his life. Let your peace make him whole."

The Holy Spirit's presence was very evident. When I said, "Amen," Ben had a massive grin on his face. He followed me downstairs.

When Ben walked back into the living room, Maggie looked at him and asked, "What happened? You're beaming."

I expected Ben to tell her about my prayers for Owen and our peace in his room. He did not. Instead, he said, "I felt heat shoot down my legs when Ivan prayed for my ankles. Look at this."

Ben rolled up his pant leg, pulled off his socks, and said, "Look, the swelling has disappeared. The swelling is gone."

Indeed, it had. Ben testified the following week in his church, comparing photos of his ankle before our prayer time with those taken that night. Everyone could see the swelling around Ben's ankle had gone down.

Owen was dry for two nights before his bed-wetting started again. While I was disappointed, I was encouraged because I had seen our prayers were making an impact.

One evening the following week, Ben and I prayed for Owen again. This time he was dry for three nights. The next time we prayed, Owen was dry for two nights. After the next time of prayer, he was dry for six nights. After wetting the bed one more time, he has been dry most nights since. Ben's accident still impacts Owen in ways we don't fully understand, but we continue to pray.

Every ministry situation is unique, and we can't assume that something we tried once will necessarily work again. However, if the Lord does lead us down the same ministry paths again, we should have tremendous confidence that we know we are operating within the boundaries of our ministry grace and faith.

It's important to note that we are not counselors. Spirit-filled counselors can play an invaluable role in helping us find freedom. But prophetic ministry is not counseling. Sometimes God reveals what is going on deep within a person so we can pray for healing, but not always. At other times, the prophetic minister, and sometimes even the person themselves, are left in the dark, and we move forward in whatever light the Lord provides.

Guard Your Heart

I'm always looking for exciting or unusual news stories or odd footage caught on video cameras. One news item that hooked me in 2022 was footage from India of a hapless security guard who fell asleep on duty while holding his gun. He accidentally shot himself. Even worse, his company's security camera captured the incident for everyone else to enjoy. Thankfully, he only suffered minor injuries to his mouth and hand, but boy, he got one loud wake-up call!

When I read Proverbs 4:23, "Above all else, guard your heart, for everything you do flows from it," I imagine two things: polluted rivers and security guards.

Let me explain. I remember reading another 2022 news article examining how upstream river pollution kills downstream fish and vegetation. It makes sense. If a hazardous chemical pollutes a river's source, it will flow downstream, killing everything it touches until it reaches the sea, where it does even more damage. Water pollution is a big problem in the US. The Clean Water Act was passed in 1972, mandating that states clean up their lakes and rivers. Sadly, a recent report reveals that more than 50 percent of lakes and rivers in the US are too polluted for swimming, fishing, or drinking.

Scripture uses the same analogy. The condition of your heart impacts every part of your life, including our prophetic ministry. If your heart pumps out the spiritual equivalent of fresh, oxidized water, you'll produce life and health. Conversely, if your heart is full of poisonous pollution, your speech will injure those you meet.

In Mark 7:20a–23, Jesus identifies the common pollutants poisoning our hearts: "What comes out of a person is what defiles them. For it is from within, out of a person's heart, that evil thoughts come—sexual immorality, theft, murder, adultery, greed, malice, deceit, lewdness, envy, slander, arrogance and folly. All these evils come from inside and defile a person."

I recall asking one of my mentors, John Steele, why I found it easier to receive words of wisdom and knowledge for strangers than for people I saw weekly in church. He told me, "Ivan, if you meet people every week, all you need to do is listen carefully to what they say. They'll tell you what's going on in their lives. Remember Luke 6:45, 'A good man brings good things out of the good stored up in his heart, and an evil man brings evil things out of the evil stored up in his heart. For the mouth speaks what the heart is full of.'"

This scripture contains pastoral advice that often makes words of knowledge unnecessary: *the mouth speaks what the heart is full of.* Just listen.

Scripture tells us that the condition of our hearts is so critical that we must act as security guards to stop junk from getting into our hearts. The problem is, like the hapless security guard from India, we have a habit of falling asleep on the job, sometimes even shooting ourselves in the process.

By and large, our society is insensitive to the destructiveness of sin. Sin destroys and pollutes not just us but others too. Corruption eats away at our insides like cancer and spreads to others like the plague. But because we don't see sin as it is, we tolerate it, control it, and live with it rather than put it to death. Only recently have scientific instruments helped us understand how the destruction of a rainforest thousands of miles away might impact the weather patterns in our backyard. We don't yet have instruments that reveal how our private sin destroys other people's lives, but God sees these connections all the time and longs to set us free.

Here's the good news: Jesus wants us to be free from sin. That's one of the outworkings of the inworking of the Holy Spirit in our lives. Paul reminds us in 2 Corinthians 3:17: "Now the Lord is the Spirit, and where the Spirit of the Lord is, there is freedom." In Galatians 5:16, Paul writes: "So I say, walk by the Spirit, and you will not gratify the desires of the flesh." If we want to be free from sin, we need to keep welcoming and fellowshipping with the person of the Holy Spirit. But we could be better at that too. We know what we need to do but fall short most days.

So, here's some more good news to encourage you. Jesus proactively hunts down the brokenness in our lives, and if we cooperate with his Spirit, he'll set us free. The more we experience personal freedom, the stronger our prophetic ministry can become.

Under the Waterfall

When I became a Jesus-follower, I needed much cleaning up. I joined the Christian Union at Aston University a few months after surrendering my life to Jesus. My friends often asked me to pray at meetings. In my youthful pride, I assumed it was because those who had been Jesus's followers for a longer time were excited to hear a new Christian pray. I'm sure that was part of it. However, it turned out that a more significant factor was that my language was crude, and the students wanted to count how many times I dropped the f-bomb in my prayers. My crudity was one of the many areas in my life Jesus would address. Thankfully, God doesn't wait for us to be whole to love us; he loves us so that we can become whole.

I was baptized in the Spirit for the first time in 1982. Not long afterward, during a time of prayer, I saw a short prophetic movie clip–style vision that would become part of my life for several years. In the vision, I could see a bedraggled man standing under a powerful waterfall. The man wore old, grubby, worn-out clothes. To keep himself dry, he held a broken umbrella over his head. I could see the water gushing through what fabric was left on the umbrella, further bending the broken spokes. The movie clip reminded me of old black-and-white Charlie Chaplin films. Who but a comic would do something so ludicrous? I soon found out.

"Ivan, this is you."

"What, Lord?"

"Ivan, this is what it is like when you try to stop my love. You can't stop my love. Many waters cannot stop my love. Let me love you. Receive my love."

I was confused. The words made no sense. I knew God loved me. I told as many as would listen about God's love.

God would not let up. Every day when I prayed and several times when I was going about my daily business, I'd see the same movie clip in my mind's eye. Every time the movie played, the Spirit impressed on me the same thing: *"Ivan, this is what it is like when you try to stop my love.*

You can't stop my love. Many waters cannot stop my love. Let me love you. Receive my love."

It dawned on me that I should respond to the vision, and I began praying about what I saw: "Lord, I don't understand what I'm missing, but help me to receive your love."

Over the course of a year, I experimented with other responses. If the man under the visionary waterfall held up his hands, I'd hold up mine, too, asking God to soak me in his love. As I mirrored what I saw in the vision, I saw the man gradually reclothed. Garment by garment, the man's attire began to change from disheveled black to glorious gold. As the vision changed, so did I. I felt lighter, less burdened, and liberated.

When the man was fully clothed in gold, he danced around the waterfall. I danced around my room, too, praying, "Lord, change me in your love."

Later, in my journal, I wrote:

> I'm learning about prophetic pictures. Remember the picture of the tramp under the waterfall, changing into glorious golden garments? I changed as I meditated on the prophetic picture each day. I can see how God is gradually healing me from the negative thoughts in my life. I'm thinking differently, but I can't quite grasp exactly what has happened. Prophetic pictures can go

> beyond giving us knowledge. Responding to the image sometimes releases the power to change us. Philippians 4:8–9 reminds us, "Finally, brothers and sisters, whatever is true, whatever is noble, whatever is right, whatever is pure, whatever is lovely, whatever is admirable—if anything is excellent or praiseworthy—think about such things. Whatever you have learned or received or heard from me, or seen in me—put it into practice. And the God of peace will be with you."

Up until this point in time, I had only ever meditated on Scripture. But I discovered through this enduring vision that the livestreams of the Holy Spirit could also be pure, lovely, right, noble, and admirable. And, as I meditated on them, God changed me.

In 2010, Kathie and I celebrated the twentieth anniversary of our first date with a trip to Argentina, where she had served as a missionary before we met. For years, Kathie had wanted to show me the Iguazu Falls, an amazing series of thunderous waterfalls bordering Argentina, Brazil, and Paraguay. We took a boat trip to one of the falls during our visit. As the boat neared the torrent of water, I thought about my vision. I wondered what it would be like to be under a waterfall. I soon found out. We were soaked. The water was far more powerful than I had anticipated. I learned something new about God's love: it is relentless, powerful, and never-ending. It soaks us. And, like our boat trip under the Iguazu Falls, once you've been drenched in God's love, you'll never forget it.

Rusty Bath

Not long after my engagement to Kathie, I was walking on the cobblestones in Trinity College's Front Square when a picture flashed into my mind. I saw an old, discarded bath, once white but now grimy gray, overflowing with junk: broken toasters, smashed TVs, computer monitors, and washing machine parts. Whenever I get these livestreams, I pause to pay attention. I looked around me. I saw art students, faculty, and tourists, and wondered if the vision was for any of them.

"That's you, Ivan. Do you really want to take that junk into your marriage?"

As I looked at the junk in the bath, I could now see words written on the broken appliances: the names of people I needed to forgive and words like *envy*, *resentment*, and *greed*. It was time to ask the Lord for a power cleanse, one that begins with the exfoliation of repentance. I wasn't sure if I had neglected to guard my heart or if God was uncovering new areas of disobedience and brokenness. What I do know is that the process of sanctification is ongoing. God never quits. He wants us holy and whole for our good and his glory.

Speak Tenderly

Directly after the New Room Conference in 2021, I flew from Nashville to San Diego. During the flight, the Lord began to impress on my heart the first two verses of Isaiah 40:

> Comfort, comfort my people,
>   says your God.
> Speak tenderly to Jerusalem,
>   and proclaim to her
> that her hard service has been completed,
>   that her sin has been paid for,
> that she has received from the LORD's hand
>   double for all her sins.

I opened the Bible Hub app on my phone and noticed that "speak tenderly" literally means "speak to the heart." Isn't that beautiful? *Prophetic ministry is speaking to the heart.*

Table Saw

Imagine for a minute you are sitting in a church service, and two thoughts come to your mind. First, you see a picture of your friend, Tyler, who's sitting on the other side of the church. After you've thought of Tyler, words come to mind: *table saw*. That's random. Unless you work with wood, you probably know nothing about table saws. If this happened to you, what would you do?

- Would you shake your head and think you're crazy, reasoning, "*Table saw* couldn't mean anything to Tyler"?
- Would you go over to your friend and shout, "Tyler, God says to you, 'table saw'"?
- Would you slip away from the service early so you wouldn't have to do anything?

This is often how the Holy Spirit gives us words of knowledge, wisdom, or prophecies. Often, the words don't make any sense to us. Try as we might, we are never sure if it's meaningful, and if so, how. We will only know if we take the risk and talk with the person.

This is what Tyler's friend did. During the ministry time at the end of the service, he walked over to Tyler and said, "Tyler, I have a word for you that I believe is from the Lord for you. I don't know what it means. It came to me just as I was sitting over there. Do the words *table saw* mean anything to you?"

Tyler's friend had no idea how Tyler would respond. The words *table saw* might be meaningless to Tyler, and his friend could be left feeling a little foolish. But the word was significant to my friend.

The day before, Tyler was installing a new kitchen floor in his first home. He had all the flooring stacked and the power tools plugged in and ready to use. His father and father-in-law had joined him to help. However, his helpers stepped in when Tyler switched on the table saw to cut the first piece of wood flooring. "You don't know how to do that properly," they told him, "and you'll only make a mess. Stand over there and let us do it for you." Tyler's father and father-in-law only wanted to help. They had laid floors before and knew what they were doing. Tyler, however, was furious. This was his house, his kitchen, and his kitchen floor. He felt humiliated and inadequate.

He was still angry when he went to church the following morning and sat fuming throughout the service. At the end of the service, he saw a friend purposely walking over to him. When his friend asked him, "Do the words *table saw* mean anything to you?" Tyler broke down in tears. The Lord then gave his friend a prophecy for Tyler: "Tyler, I want you to know that the Creator of the universe sees you and understands you. He thinks you are enough."

This tender ministry would never have happened if Tyler's friend had remained silent. Tyler has been my friend for many years, and he still tells this story. God used Tyler's friend to minister to his brokenness. However, the impact of that word has lasted for years and reminds Tyler that a tenderhearted God loves him.

Heart Massage

One of my current joys and responsibilities is to help prepare ministerial candidates in my denomination for Holy Spirit ministry. During one training session, I had a prophetic vision for a ministerial candidate who felt overwhelmed by the pressure of work and new responsibilities. Here's what I saw in this vision: I saw the ministerial candidate in a hospital operating theater. Jesus, his surgeon, had his hands inside the pastor's chest cavity, massaging his heart. If you've ever seen an emergency room TV series like *Grey's Anatomy* in the US or *Casualty* in the UK, you can imagine the scene. In the TV series, you'd see the surgeon standing, looking worried, with sweat pouring from their brow. You hope the patient will live, but you're not quite sure. The scene I saw wasn't like this at all. Jesus wasn't panicking. He had no sweat running from his brow. He looked calm. Jesus looked up at me and said, "Don't worry. I won't get tired. I can keep this up for as long as he needs."

So here's the good news: Jesus doesn't only speak tenderly to our hearts, he massages our tired, weary hearts too. And he is saying the same thing to you and me right now as he said to my young pastor friend: *Don't worry. I won't get tired. I can keep this up for as long as you need.*

Your Turn

If you go to the movies, you'll know we are near the end. The picture is about to fade, the credits will roll, and the cleaners will shortly come into the movie theater to clean up your popcorn mess! My story is but one part of a series, and the Holy Spirit wants to cast you in his next real-life drama. I wrote this book to prepare you for your role. You have learned that the Holy Spirit can cast anyone—even you. You understand some ministry safeguards, so you can play your part safely. Activation exercises and spiritual forensics will help you connect with the Director, and the reward will be out of this world. Are you ready?

Lights, camera, ACTION!

Questions for Reflection and Discussion

1. How do you guard your heart? What advice can you give to others?

2. What are some ways the Lord uses to show you what is going on in the depths of your heart?

3. Meditate on this thought: *I want you to know that the Creator of the universe sees you and understands you. He thinks you are enough.* What thoughts and emotions bubble up? Bring these thoughts and feelings to the Lord in prayer.

4. Imagine yourself standing under the waterfall of God's love. Let him wash you clean as you get drenched. Bring him all your fears, concerns, questions, and doubts, and let his love wash over you. See what happens.

5. Imagine Jesus has his hands in your chest cavity and is tenderly massaging your heart. In your imagination, what is Jesus saying to you? How can you respond to his words?

Printed by Libri Plureos GmbH in Hamburg, Germany

9 798888 000755